NOT THE WEST HIGHLAND WAY: A MOUNTAIN HIGH WAY

MOUNTAIN ALTERNATIVES AND BACKPACKING IDEAS TO LINK WITH THE WEST HIGHLAND WAY

by Ronald Turnbull

JUNIPER HOUSE, MURLEY MOSS,
OXENHOLME ROAD, KENDAL, CUMBRIA LA9 7RL
www.cicerone.co.uk

© Ronald Turnbull 2025
Second edition 2025
ISBN: 978 1 78631 187 0
eISBN: 978 1 78765 090 9
First edition 2010

Printed in Czechia on responsibly sourced paper on behalf of Latitude Press Ltd.
A catalogue record for this book is available from the British Library.
All photographs are by the author unless otherwise stated.

Route mapping by Lovell Johns
www.lovelljohns.com

© Crown copyright 2025 OS AC0000810376. NASA relief data courtesy of ESRI

Updates to this guide

While every effort is made by our authors to ensure the accuracy of guidebooks as they go to print, changes can occur during the lifetime of an edition. Any updates that we know of for this guide will be on the Cicerone website (www.cicerone.co.uk/1187/updates), so please check before planning your trip. We also advise that you check information about such things as transport, accommodation and shops locally. Even rights of way can be altered over time. We are always grateful for information about any discrepancies between a guidebook and the facts on the ground, sent by email to updates@cicerone.co.uk.

Register your book: To sign up to receive free updates, special offers and GPX files where available, create a Cicerone account and register your purchase via the 'My Account' tab at www.cicerone.co.uk.

Front cover: Old stalkers' path through the Mamores above Kinlochleven (Route 12)

CONTENTS

Overview of routes (south to north) 6
Route summary table 12

INTRODUCTION 15
The high road and the low 15
When to go 19
Safety in the mountains 21
Maps 22
Using this guide 23
A winter Not the West Highland Way 25

PART ONE: THE HIGH ROAD AND THE LOW 31

Milngavie to Drymen 32
1   Hill Option: the Campsie Fells 35

Drymen to Rowardennan 38

Rowardennan to Inversnaid 41
2   Rowardennan Outing: Ben Lomond 43
3   Hill Crossing: Ben Lomond to Inversnaid 48

Inversnaid to Inverarnan 51
4   Hill Crossing: Beinn a' Choin 53
5   Inverarnan Outing: Beinn Chabhair 56

Inverarnan to Tyndrum 58
6   Hill Crossing: Ben Lui 61
7   Crianlarich Outing: An Caisteal and Beinn a' Chroin 66

Tyndrum to Inveroran 70
8   Hill Crossing: the back of Beinn Dorain 72
9   Inveroran Outing: Ben Inverveigh and Meall Tairbh 76

Inveroran to Kings House 79
10 Hill Crossing: Black Mount 82

Kings House to Kinlochleven 88
11   Hill Crossing: Beinn a' Chrulaiste and the Blackwater. 90

Kinlochleven to Fort William 94
12   Hill Crossing: Mamores 97
13   Hill Crossing: Between the Binneins 104
14   Fort William Outing: Ben Nevis by the CMD Arête 110

PART TWO: BEGINNERISH BACKPACKING 115
The excitement is in tents 118
Midges are unpleasant 120
May is the month 121
Shoulder-strengthening short trips... 123
The off-route food-fetching formula 123
Stuff, stuffsacks, and throwing it all away 124

15   A mostly gentle two-day: the back of Ben Nevis 134
16   A wilder two-day: Taynuilt to Bridge of Orchy. 141

PART 3: AWAY FROM THE WAY 149
17   Dumbarton Start. 152
18   Wrong side of the loch: the Arrochar Alps 158
19   The Etive Trek 169
20   Blackwater and the Lairig Leacach 178
21   Routes of Rannoch 186

The author bivvying on Pillar, Lake District

PART 4: ROADS TO THE DEEP NORTH 195
22 Corrour to Dalwhinnie 198
23 Fort William to Inverie 201
24 Spean Bridge to Cluanie and even Cape Wrath. 207

Appendix A: Access 212
Appendix B: Useful information 215
Appendix C: Further reading. 217

Warning

Mountain walking can be a dangerous activity carrying a risk of personal injury or death. It should be undertaken only by those with a full understanding of the risks and with the training and experience to evaluate them. While every care and effort has been taken in the preparation of this guide, the user should be aware that conditions can be highly variable and can change quickly, materially affecting the seriousness of a mountain walk. Therefore, except for any liability which cannot be excluded by law, neither Cicerone nor the author accept liability for damage of any nature (including damage to property, personal injury or death) arising directly or indirectly from the information in this book.

To call out the Mountain Rescue, ring 999 or the international emergency number 112: this will connect you via any available network. Once connected to the emergency operator, ask for Police Scotland.

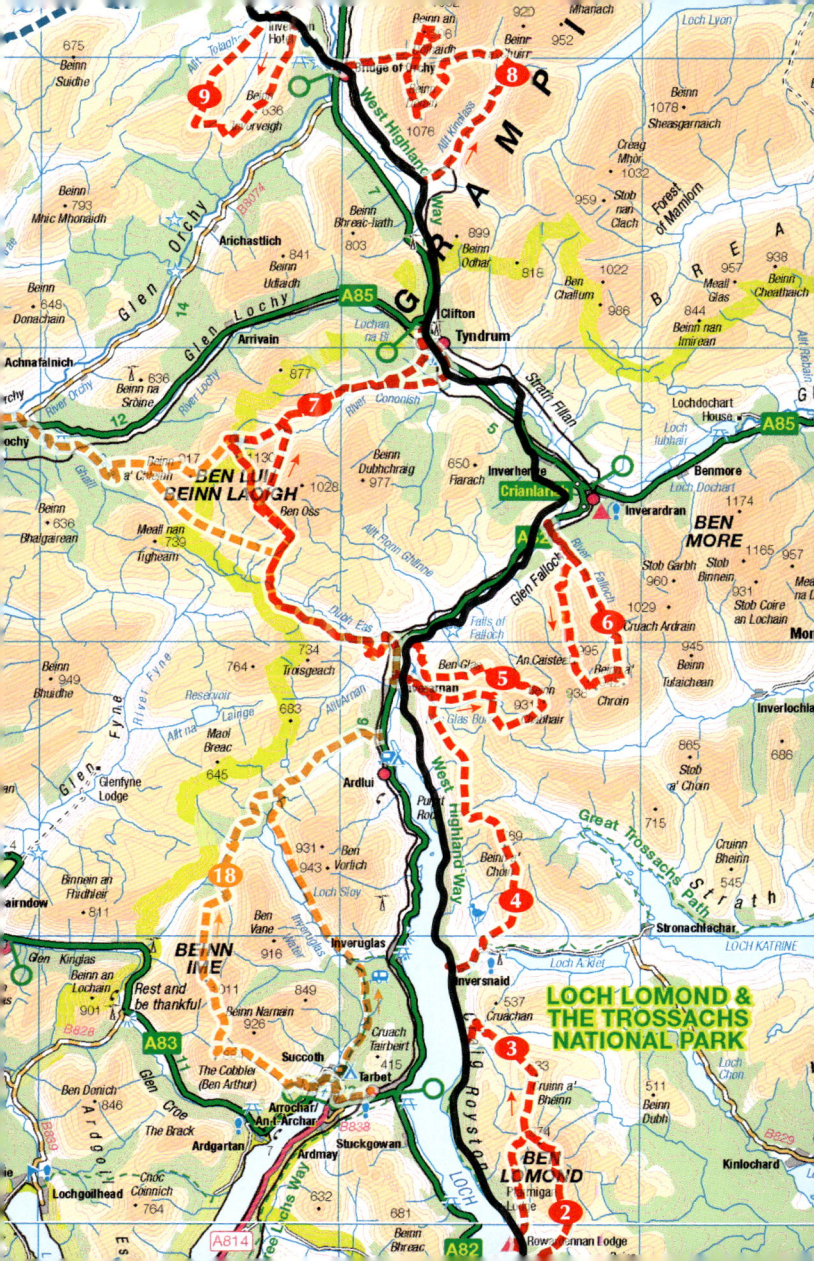

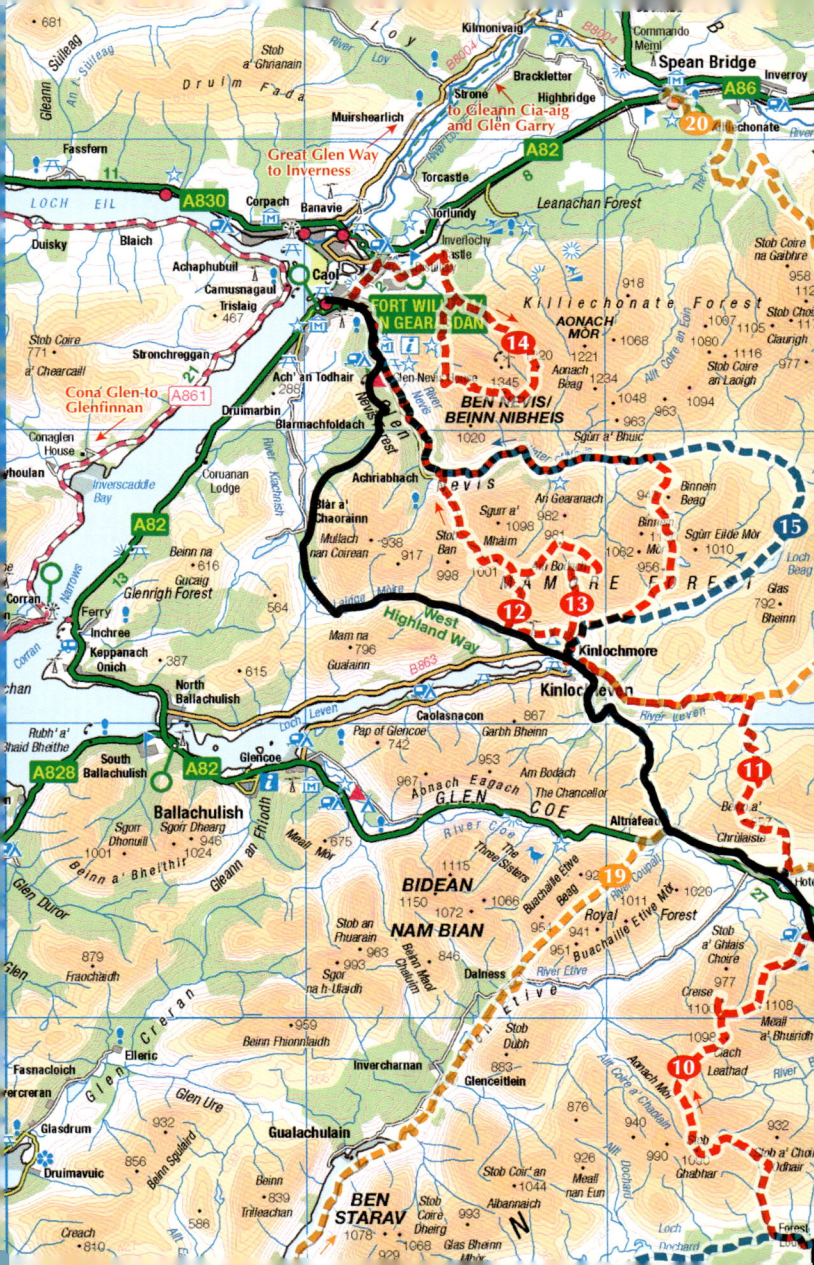

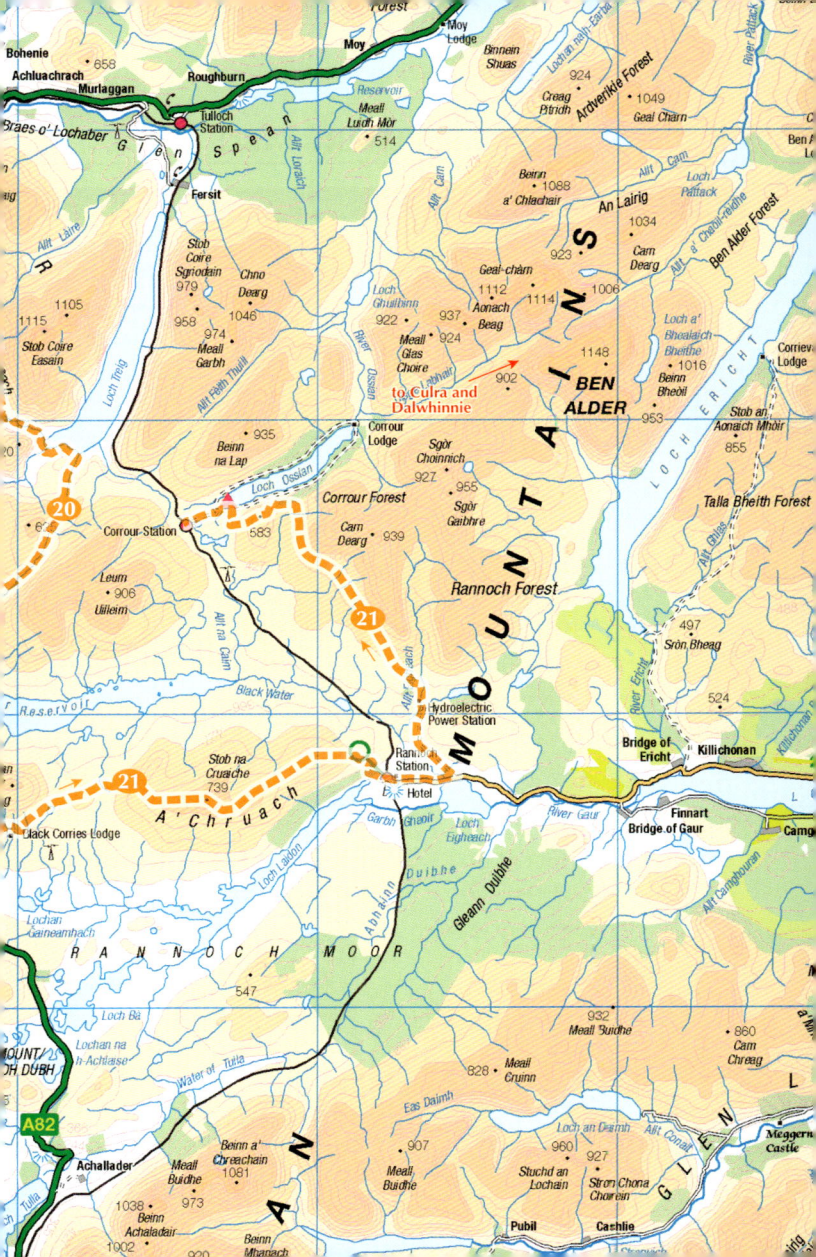

NOT THE WEST HIGHLAND WAY: A MOUNTAIN HIGH WAY

ROUTE SUMMARY TABLE

Part	Route		Start	Finish
Part One	1	Campsie Fells	Milngavie	Drymen
	2	Ben Lomond	Rowardennan	Rowardennan
	3	Ben Lomond crossing	Rowardennan	Inversnaid
	4	Beinn a' Choin	Inversnaid	Inverarnan
	5	Beinn Chabhair	Inverarnan	Inverarnan
	6	Ben Lui high pass	Inverarnan	Tyndrum
	7	An Caisteal and Beinn a' Chroin	Crianlarich	Crianlarich
	8	Back of Beinn Dorain	Tyndrum	Bridge of Orchy
	9	Ben Inverveigh	Inveroran	Inveroran
	10	Black Mount	Inveroran	Kings house
	11	Beinn a' Chrulaiste	Kings House	Kinlochleven
	12	Mamores	Kinlochleven	Fort William
	13	Between the Binneins	Kinlochleven	Ft William YH
	14	Ben Nevis	Fort William	Fort William
Part Two	15	Back of Ben Nevis	Kings House	Fort William
	16	Taynuilt to Bridge of Orchy	Taynuilt	Bridge of Orchy
Part Three	17	Dumbarton Start	Dumbarton	Drymen
	18	Arrochar Alps	Arrochar	Inverarnan
	19	Etive Trek	Inverarnan	Kings House
	20	Blackwater & Lairig Leacach	Kinlochleven	Spean Bridge
	21	Routes of Rannoch	Kings House	Corrour Station
Part Four	22	Corrour to Dalwhinnie	Corrour Station	Dalwhinnie
	23	Fort William to Inverie	Fort William (ferry)	Inverie
	24	Spean Bridge to Cluanie and even Cape Wrath	Spean Bridge	Cluanie

ROUTE SUMMARY TABLE

Type	Distance (km)	Ascent (m)	Time (hr)	Page
ill crossing	29	850	9	35
ill circuit	10.5	1050	5	43
ill crossing	18	1200	7	48
ill crossing	14	1000	6	53
ill circuit	15.5	1350	7	56
igh pass	22	750	7	61
ill circuit	21.5	1250	8	66
ill crossing	24.5	1300	9	72
ill circuit	12	650	4.5	76
ill crossing	22.5	1600	9	82
ill crossing	16	650	5.5	90
ill crossing	20.5	1000	7.5	97
igh passes	24	850	8.5	104
ill circuit	23	1500	9	110
-day backpack	50	800	14 (two days)	134
-day backpack	40	400	11 (one and a half days)	141
ill crossing	30.5	650	9	152
ill crossing	25	1550	9.5	158
-4 day backpack	79	2800	24 (three days)	169
-day backpack	40	700	12 (a long day and a short day)	178
-day backpack	36.5	1050	12 (two short days)	186
igh pass	37	400	10 (two short days)	198
near multi-day	80	1800	24 (three days)	201
near multi-day	depends on route choice	depends on route choice	depends on route choice	207

The other way to Fort William: the book's first backpack, Route 15, passes Steall Waterfall on its way down Glen Nevis

INTRODUCTION

West Highland Way on Telford's road across Rannoch Moor, with Black Mount hills Clach Leathad and Meall a' Bhuiridh (Route 10)

THE HIGH ROAD AND THE LOW

The West Highland Way is one of the finest, if not *the* finest, of Britain's long-distance paths. It passes through six separate mountain ranges, from the tall cone of Ben Lomond and the crag towers of grim Glen Coe, to the seductive Mamores. It runs from Scotland's largest city, alongside her longest loch, by way of the biggest and bleakest patch of peaty moorland, to the foot of her highest mountain, paralleled in its path by (as it happens) the Highlands' second busiest main road and also the West Highland Railway.

The comfortable gravel path, the well-placed waymarks and cosy bunkhouses, the cheerful evening singer doing (yet again) Loch Lomond's 'bonnie banks': do these really compensate for not going up any of those mountains? Not when above the stony path there rises the compelling cone of Beinn Dorain, sprinkled at its top with snow. So instead of sticking to the path I wandered up the Auch Gleann and bagged Beinn Dorain from the back, leaving the West Highland Way, over three miles to Bridge of Orchy, technically unwalked.

For those new to the Highlands and the big hills, the WH Way is a dream – and a convenient dream, with its signposts and bridges, its hostels and its shops. But for those more familiar with the hills, it's a shop itself: a sweetie shop – and you haven't any pennies in your pocket. For all of those fine mountains are seen, yes, but you're not allowed to touch.

As Capt Edward Burt recorded in 1765, of the military road that's now the WH Way: 'The objections made by some among the Highlanders are that the bridges in particular will render the ordinary people effeminate.' And it's happened. It may be Scotland's best long-distance path: but this book intends to do a great deal better.

Part One takes the line that you're walking the route of the conventional WH Way, and using its overnight stops; but during the days you divert onto a mountain alongside. When the clouds are down you stay down as well, and walk the official footpath. But when the sun shines, and the twitter of the skylarks is somehow more appealing than the rumble of the A82, here are Ben Lomond and Beinn Dorain, the charming Campsie Fells, and the mighty Mamores; and the best pub-to-pub in these islands, the high-level crossing of the Black Mount from Inveroran to Glen Coe. This is the WH Way idea – the same WH Way overnights, the pre-booked bunkhouse, the luggage transfer service – but higher excitements.

Not all of those excitements are the ever-popular Munros. The first is the Lowland range of the Campsie Fells, rising to a mere 578m. Two later ones aren't tops at all, but high mountain passes: through the Lui group, and then over the Mamores. Another two are the lesser, and less-visited, hills called Corbetts. And even on popular Ben Lomond you're not just bagging it and coming back. You're crossing Ben Lomond to distant Inversnaid, and this takes you onto the grassy northern ridgeline where it's just you, the view, and some skylarks high above Loch Lomond.

Part One's four hill outings are simple Munro-bagging. Why not? A well-walked-on path, a satisfying horseshoe route, a number of like-minded people coming up alongside. Plus the convenience of returning to your start point, where the damp clothes of last night have had time to dry, there's no shopping to do because you shopped for two days yesterday, the bed is still warm from the night before. Those too stingy to use the baggage transfer, in particular, can enjoy the lighter rucksack of the circular day walk.

To qualify as a true Not the WH Way, four or more of the high lines have to be taken, excluding the circular outings. There are eight to choose from: the Campsie Fells (or alternatively the Dumbarton start, Route 17); the crossing of Ben Lomond to Inversnaid; Beinn a' Choin; Ben Lui's high pass or else its summit; Beinn Dorain's back way; the Black Mount Traverse; Beinn a' Chrulaiste and Blackwater; and the

On the south ridge of Ben Lomond (Routes 2 and 3), looking to the tops of the Arrochar Alps (Route 18)

Mamores crossing (or alternatively the Glen Nevis backpack, Route 15). Those who use this book for the circular excursions, along with three or fewer of the off-path diversions, don't complete the official Not the WH Way. They have achieved what we have to call a 'Not the Not the West Highland Way'.

When you start walking you hold onto your mummy's hand. When you start walking the rather longer distances with the big rucksack, the mummy is the West Highland Way. It tells you where to go, it makes sure you've got somewhere safe to spend the night, it cooks your tea, it even fusses about trying to keep your socks dry. Then as you start to grow up it lets you wander off out of sight – but you'd better be back by teatime.

Grown-ups don't want to be home in time for tea. Grown-ups stay out late and get into the nightlife. We want to drop our packs under a pylon-free sky, look around and see no street lights, sniff and smell heather – not petrol. We want to gather stones to shelter the stove, and hang our socks in the tree by the river. We want to watch from the high corrie of Ben Lui, as 40 mountains go grey and purplish against an orange sky.

In Part One, the use of the WH Way's overnight stops and baggage transfer allows backpacking, as it were, but without the backpack. When Part Two attempts your first two-day tent adventure, the ground alongside the Way turns out to be just grand for that as well. There is genuine wild country in the southwest Highlands,

NOT THE WEST HIGHLAND WAY: A MOUNTAIN HIGH WAY

The Cobbler and Loch Lomond (Route 18)

hikes designed to get you going on this game of carrying the big rucksack along the valleys and through between the hills. Learn how to do it not by deep study of the literature, but by doing it, and doing it wrong. Discover for yourself the setting up of a damp camp when you've been walking in the rain for four hours. Find out that you should have put your dry pants in a plastic bag. And if you did manage to forget the tent pegs, there's a bothy alongside to crawl into with the sodden sleeping bag, and a train home tomorrow so that the suffering is at least reasonably short.

Part Three is the proposition that Glasgow (or Loch Lomond) to Fort William is one of Scotland's good walks, so simply ignore the WH Way altogether. Here are the damp little paths along Loch Etive, and the peaty ways through the heart of Rannoch Moor.

After two days of waterfalls and windswept heather, come down to Kinlochleven (say), do your shopping, eat a big hot meal plus sticky toffee, stay in the hostel there. Set out again at dawn, or whenever you manage to get out of bed (let's hope it's quite early). At the back of Kinlochleven is a wooded valley. Waterfalls splash down into a river that zigzags across slabs of bare rock. Walk up the slippery stone path below the birches and the oaks. After four miles you come up to this bleak, bleak reservoir, the Blackwater. You find the old path through the peat, and you come to a lochan, and beside

between Loch Lomond and Lochaber: big beautiful valleys with craggy mountains rising on either side. But there's also a pretty good path, there are bothies, there is that bus stop for Glasgow just one day's walk ahead. Corrour railway station stands at the geometrical centre of nowhere at all: it has a café, and a youth hostel, but not a road leading to it.

So Part Two has tips for beginner backpackers. And after the tips, the trips: a couple of two-day it there's a beautiful bothy that hardly anybody uses, as it's not really on the way to anywhere. But if a roof of any sort is repugnant, you can carry on and camp beside the water. All night the ripples murmur against the stones. And at four in the morning, the curlews are crying in the air above your tent.

The fairly good path continues for a couple of hours, through a heathery slot in the hills. It's Gleann Iolairean, Eagle Valley. You might see that eagle soaring overhead; you'll almost certainly see some ravens. Come out to the next big reservoir. Now if you turn left, it's up along a stony stream with waterfalls, and alder trees, and grassy riverbanks for the path; then gradually down again as you're now in Glen Nevis. You walk below big Ben Nevis on one side, the shapely Mamores range on the other. The heather gets denser, the river bigger, and the air gets slightly cosier as you lose height. Suddenly you're in the meadow at the glen's end, with the Steall Waterfall tumbling over grey quartzite, and the great tree-hung Nevis Gorge. Then it's out to the youth hostel for another big meal.

If the twined-together routes of Parts One to Three are the stalk, then Part Four is the flower. As the train clatters south across Rannoch Moor, your feet are sore but your head is filling up with ideas. Outwards and onwards lies the whole of the Scottish Highlands.

The West Highland Way, with its well-made path, its centuries of history, its mountain surroundings, is the best long path in Scotland. But the best is just the beginning. Here's the follow-on: which is 'Not the West Highland Way'.

WHEN TO GO

April is still winter on the summits, but down in the glen the WH Way path offers good walking then and in May. The leaves are breaking, the birds are busy, and the midges are harmless larvae lurking in the bog. At these off-season times the busy footpath can be almost deserted – I walked it at the end of March and met four other parties. Youth hostels of SYHA may be shut but the independent ones are open all year round, and at quiet times you probably don't need to book in advance.

Meanwhile, the mountaintops above may be suffering sleet and hail, and be covered in soggy wet snow. On the other hand, the air may be clear and crisp, with sunshine on the white top of Ben Nevis. So walk the path if it's wet, and if the sun comes out, hit the heights.

May and June are enjoyable at all altitudes. These are the least rainy months in the Highlands; the leaves are fresh and green; there are 18 daylight hours, enough for even the most energetic. The one annoyance can be the cuckoos, mocking you as you go.

July and August can be hot and humid, with less rewarding views. This is also when the WH Way path is at its busiest, and midges are at their most vigorous, infesting the glens. The last two weeks in August do bring out the best of the heather – although there are no really huge heather moors on the WH Way.

Midges hang on until the first frost, normally some time in September. October often brings clear air and lovely autumn colour. The woodland along Loch Lomond can be excellent as the birch leaves turn gold (the third week in October being the ideal moment in most years). More surprisingly, Rannoch Moor goes orange all over. In between times there'll be gales.

The red deer are being shot at from the middle of August until 21 October. The West Highland Way itself is a right of way, as are almost all the backpacking routes in Parts Two and Three (blue and orange on the overview maps). Many of the hill routes in Part One welcome walkers year-round, but a handful do have limitations on access during the three autumn months (see Appendix A).

Winter is a time of short days and often foul weather. Snow lies on the high tops from December to April, with patches in the corries obstructing some routes even into May. Few will attempt the routes in this book during the cold months. Those who do could just enjoy crisp cramponing along the ridges, views of hundreds of mountains, and buttercup-coloured sunsets; such a journey is described later in this Introduction.

West Highland Way, above River Falloch

SAFETY IN THE MOUNTAINS

In the glens of Part Three you can be a day's walk from the nearest road or habitation, and without a mobile phone signal. In the mountains, especially north of Rannoch Moor, the ground you need to get off by may be steep with crags. Safety and navigation in the mountains is best learnt from companions, experience, and perhaps a paid instructor; such instruction is outside the scope of this book.

Most of the routes and outings in Part One are no more than moderately serious, and a walker used to day walks in the Lake District or Snowdonia should feel at home on them. The main difference is that in various places, Part One takes you off the trodden paths. This can be disconcerting or worse if you are unhappy with your navigation.

The international mountain distress signal is some sign (shout, whistle, torch flash or other) repeated six times over a minute, followed by a minute's silence. The reply is a sign repeated three times over a minute, followed by a minute's silence. To signal for help from a helicopter, raise both arms above your head and then drop them down sideways, repeatedly. If you're not in trouble, don't shout or whistle on the hills, and don't wave to passing helicopters.

To call out the mountain rescue, phone 999 from a landline. From a mobile, phone either 999 or the international emergency number 112: these will connect you via any available network. Reception is good on most summits and ridges, but absent in places without direct sightlines to settlements such as Bridge of Orchy, or to the mast behind Kings House. Sometimes a text message can get through when a voice call can't; to register your phone and enable 999 text messages visit www.emergencysms.co.uk.

Given the unreliable phone coverage, it is wise to leave word of your proposed route with some responsible person (and, of course, tell that person when you've safely returned). Youth hostels have specific forms for this, as do many independent hostels and B&Bs. You could also leave word at the police stations at Glencoe or Fort William.

Being lost or tired is not sufficient reason for calling the rescue service, and neither, in normal summer weather, is being benighted. However, team members I've talked to say not to be too shy about calling them: they greatly prefer bringing down bodies that are still alive…

There is no charge for mountain rescue in Scotland – teams are voluntary, financed by donations from the public, with a grant from the Scottish Executive and helicopters from His Majesty's Coastguard and the Scottish Air Ambulance. You can make donations at youth hostels, tourist information centres and many pubs.

NOT THE WEST HIGHLAND WAY: A MOUNTAIN HIGH WAY

MAPS

The West Highland Way is a wide, well-used path, or else a vehicle track, and is well waymarked. For anyone aiming for nothing more than the mere path, even the cheapest map will do. That cheapest map is produced by Footprint, at about £5. The best map of the path is Harveys West Highland Way at 1:40,000 scale. It's printed on tough polythene, has proper contour lines, and covers a wide enough strip to include Ben Lomond (Routes 2 and 3), the Mamores crossing (Route 12) and the less interesting route up Ben Nevis.

For long hikes through the back country, you need a map that not only shows that back country but also the ground around – in case you wander into that ground and get lost (or more cheeringly if you're inspired to wider explorations than originally planned). The very useful Harvey British Mountain Map series is at 1:40,000. 'Southern Highlands' covers the area from Rowardennan on Loch Lomond to Tyndrum. 'Ben Nevis' continues northwards, from Inveroran and the head of Loch Etive, with the exception of Route 21 to Rannoch Station. The map is printed on polythene so robust that one outdoor writer uses it as his groundsheet.

Second best is still more than good enough. The Ordnance Survey's Landranger series at 1:50,000 covers the whole area, and indeed the whole of the UK. It is well surveyed, clear and easy to read. It has two minor drawbacks. Even on a brand new map, the information on forestry plantations and forest roads is liable to be a decade or two out of date. And the footpaths marked are proscriptive rather than descriptive, which is a fancy way of saying they mark paths that ought (for historical or other

reasons) to exist, rather than the ones that actually do. Sheets 64 (Glasgow), 56 (Loch Lomond), 50 (Glen Orchy) and 41 (Ben Nevis) cover the ground – almost. You need Sheet 57 (Stirling) for Drymen on the WH Way, but not for any of the 'Not the WH Way' routes. And the Rannoch crossing (Route 21) requires Sheet 42 (Glen Garry) as well as Sheet 41.

For exploration of crags and corries and pathless boulder slopes, you would be helped by the extra contour detail at 1:25,000 scale. The routes in this book don't require this extra bulk and expense. However, for those who insist that bigger is invariably better, there is the 1:25,000 Explorer series of the Ordnance Survey. This is excellent mapping apart from the fact that many of the summits are so obscured with crag-marks that the contour detail is almost illegible. If you're prepared to pay extra for a map that's printed on waterproof paper, and marks paths where they actually are, most (but not all) of the routes are on various 1:25,000 Superwalker sheets from Harveys.

A compass is a very useful aid in mist, even if your skills only extend to 'northwest, southeast' rather than precision bearings. Magnetic deviation is effectively zero in the UK through the 2020s. No magnetic rocks have been found in this area (it's you that's wrong, not the compass!).

If using a phone for navigation, the OS Maps app is one good way to access suitable mapping. Be sure to preload the necessary map bits into your phone, and carry a backup battery pack.

USING THIS GUIDE

The headers at the start of each walk should be self-explanatory. The approximate times are based on one

Beinn Dorain and Auch Gleann (Route 8) with Beinn a' Chaisteal and Beinn Odhar; the WH Way runs along the base of the hills

NOT THE WEST HIGHLAND WAY: A MOUNTAIN HIGH WAY

hour for four horizontal km or for 500m of height gained, with extra time where the ground is particularly steep or rough. They'll be about right, including snack stops, for a moderately fast party with light rucksacks, or a strong one backpacking.

Within Part One, in between the Not the West Highland Way's numbered routes (hill crossings and circular outings), there are brief descriptions of the actual WH Way, for use in case of tiredness or nasty weather.

For the linear routes of Parts Two and Three, the headers include notes on public transport to and from the end-points, and, if there should be any, of facilities such as shops available on the way. The WH Way itself is splendidly equipped with hostels, campsites, bus stops and shops; these are listed in Appendix B, along with general public transport information.

In old numbers, 600ft was a vertical distance, while 200yd was horizontal. I've used a similar convention, so that 600m is an altitude, or a height gain, while 600 metres (with 'etres') is along the ground. I use 'track' (rather than 'path') for a way wide enough for a tractor or Landrover.

Buachaille Etive Mor and Beinn a' Chrulaiste from the track to Black Corries Lodge (Route 21)

A WINTER NOT THE WEST HIGHLAND WAY

The Not the West Highland Way idea is less perverse than it sounds. Ever since the path was opened walkers have been taking in Ben Lomond, and using Ben Nevis as a post-walk warm-down. Many more will have walked under Beinn Dorain, gazed longingly upwards, and wished they'd brought along the extra map and hadn't already scheduled themselves forward to Inveroran. When I stopped on my own WH Way walk at Tyndrum's By the Way Hostel, I wasn't terribly surprised to see the squiggly line painted across its ceiling that is the altitude profile for 'The Highland High Way', a Not the WHW that's a whole lot more strenuous than anything in this book, invented in 1996 by two tough types called Heather Connon and Paul Roper.

Indeed, the usual response to Not the West Highland Way isn't so much 'Not the what?' as 'Oh I did that *ages*

South ridge of Binnein Mor

ago.' My friend David Didn't the West Highland Way in May 1990, under 'more snow than I was planning on for a solo trip'. David enjoyed all four of the Black Mount Munros before a night at Kings House with a disconcerting waterbed effect under his tent as the 'bathtub-type' sewn-in groundsheet operated as the name suggests (except with the water being on the *outside*). He continued, much more energetically than anything in this book, over Buachaille Etive Mor, the sky-piercing scramble of the Aonach Eagach, and nine of the Mamores.

As for me, Not the WH Way swam into my mind in 1993 in response to a phone call from eastern Europe at an unexpected time of the year. 'I have time off from the shop',

---

Route symbols on OS map extracts

〜〜 route
〜〜 alternative route
🚶 start/finish point
🚶 start point
🚶 finish point
◀ route direction

For OS symbols key see OS maps

GPX files for all routes can be downloaded free at www.cicerone.co.uk/1187/GPX.

said Alois my Czech friend. 'How is Scotland in February?'

February is not necessarily Scotland's best. So I planned a five-day journey for minimum misery. Loch Lomond to Fort William offers pubs, hostels and shops. There are plentiful escapes by cosy Citylink and Scotrail. There's a path alongside Loch Etive that's been on my Landranger for the last ten years without my doing anything about it. And at worst, there's a heavy-rucksacked trudge up the West Highland Way with the sleet, quite possibly, coming from behind.

But the best-laid plans of mice and mountaineers... Something happened to throw the whole scheme into confusion. It was, as always, the weather. To our shock and surprise, the sun came out.

So it was that we found ourselves on a route that, by Day 3, was to be Not the West Highland Way by a span of about 20 miles sideways.

There's a lot to be said for using Inverarnan, Inveroran, all the WH Way's orthodox overnight stops; and looking upwards each day at the weather, downwards at the legs, and deciding between the well-built path and the mountain excitements alongside. And if that's your idea at the moment, you'll skip a few pages down to Part One, rather than reading of how my Czech mate and I hauled rather large rucksacks up the Cobbler on what will, later in this book, be Route 18. You won't want to know how we almost needed our

Alois rests above Kinlochleven

crampons up there, except that the people before us had left hippo-size footsteps in the snow. Cloud was wafting around the three rocky tops, and forming beautiful hoarfrost over them. We stood and admired the beautiful hoarfrost. We weren't tempted to climb through the hoarfrosted hole, along the hoarfrosted ledge, and onto the exciting true top of the Cobbler.

'What's this thing on the back of the ice-axe?' Alois asked. Ah, the adze! Nailed boots and the noble art of step-cutting, that's the proper way. Step-cutting is slow but satisfying, but even more fun is to scamper in crampons across crisp Beinn Ime like a wasp on a wedding cake. Then we dropped off to the north, wandered along a boggy valley and down a damp birchwood. They let us camp at Beinglas campsite even though it was closed, and in the night my boots froze to two rigid lumps.

In the morning the sun was shining. Alois the Czech was astonished, as he knew it doesn't do that in Scotland two days in a row. But since it was, we branched off again to the west – Route 19. We cramponed up Ben Lui, and watched the climbers pop one behind the other out of the top of Central Gully, quite like the computer game of *Lemmings* except that they didn't walk off vertically down the other side but came and sat down at the cairn.

Wandering to west of the West Highland Way meant no bunkhouses or hostels: but with the shiny sun alternating with cloudless moon, we could tent it the three days to Kinlochleven. 'Ah, but I have a slightly sore leg,' said Alois. 'A hot shower would be the thing.'

Well, there might conceivably be a B&B in Dalmally. And the B&B might even be open, supposing we ignored the fact that most places do close in February. And so, going down the forest track, we discussed the maximum we'd pay for the treat of trickling hot water on the leg. In the High Tatras (circa 2003), £9 buys a hotel room for two plus use of the swimming pool.

In Dalmally, a small sign nailed to a phone pole indicates a B&B that charges £3 less even than our stingy maximum, offers not just shower but bath, and extra towels to dry the

Argyll Needle, the summit of the Cobbler

tent with. Breakfast is full fry with haggis – happily, two days over Ime and Lui have created the appetite to cope. 'Going to Glen Etive? A nice run that, but roundabout,' says helpful Mr B&B. 'You'll have to go right back to Tyndrum, then across the Moor.' Our big boots and damp tent are just a tease. Obviously we have a car parked round the corner...

Our way to Glen Etive is slower than the road, but straighter. An invisible stalkers' path through a high pass, a riverside track down Glen Kinglass, and then that little dashed line along Loch Etive. The Etive path exists just enough to be followable. Bog, stones, and grassy foreshore: but the freeze is right down to the sea and the wet bits are slide-over-bump rather than in-squelch. Gradually we trekked past Beinn Trilleachan, with the famous Trilleachan slabs icy grey under low cloud. We found a sheltered corner at the head of the loch; it didn't snow or even rain; and the covering cloud kept us nice and cosy. Above us on Ben Starav, a waterfall made soothing noises all night long.

In the morning the sun was shining yet again. (Who wants the Highlands in February, eh?) We zigzagged arduously up the end of Buachaille Beag. The smaller Buachaille is just one of many fine mountains apparent on the map but not mentioned in the body of this book because there are just so many of them.

Buachaille Beag's a logical extension for anyone with spare energy on this part of Route 18. We made scratchy crampon noises all along its lovely ridge, to find a way down northwest from just short of its final summit Stob nan Cabar. Luckily we were walking away from the sunshine; sunscreen was one burden I hadn't thought to bring. Then up the Devil's Staircase, and there was the Pap of Glencoe standing erect against the afternoon.

One more range stands between us and journey's end. Except that, in Scotland's winter, you do have to adapt your plans to the weather. And extreme weather is on the way: yet another day of winter chill and cloudless blue skies. When sun runs golden along this particular range, you can't just ignore the Mamores. We booked at Blackwater Hostel for a second night, hung the tent in the drying room, and clicked and scratched our way up the steep end of Binnein Mor.

When I was in the Western Tatras, they rather reminded me of the Mamores. Narrow ridges with wide paths, steep drops alongside, down the ridge and up the ridge and here's another pointy peak. (The High Tatras, which are granite, are something else again.) What do you think, Alois? Tatric a bit?

The Tatras may be twice as high but, Alois explained carefully, Scotland is still much bigger for him. 'In Scotland if you look around you see only mountains and mountains, I really love this. Also the beautiful

On Stob Dubh of Buachaille Etive Beag

lochs.' Indeed, with chill sub-zero air, a sharp snow edge, Loch Leven below and a view from Mull to Schiehallion, it's no trouble at all to forget about Scotland's bog, our grey rain, our miserable summer midges.

A sharp dip leads into the cleavage between the twin peaks of Na Gruagaichean, 'The Maidens'. The col is steep in and steep out, with verticality on the right, but in this superb snow the crampons can cope. On the second top we looked at birds against the blue sky. No, not an eagle: a raven. Corvus something, sorry I don't know the Latin.

'I know raven,' said Alois: 'Quoth the Raven, Nevermore.' Edgar Allen Poe is big in Moravia.

On over the easy Munro of Stob Coire a' Chairn; and now the white mountains against blue were being buzzed round by a little yellow helicopter. The 'copter made figure eights, Scottish-dance style, round each of the summits. It seemed to be searching for someone whose route plan had been an unhelpful 'Mamores'. We ignored it and looked at Am Bodach. Am Bodach is translated as 'old man'. Actually it's the particular sort of old man you scare your babies with, the old bloke that if they carry on like that will come down the chimney when they're asleep and get them. The climb to Am Bodach is, in summer, steep and awkward scree. Now it was hard snow, still steep, among rocky outcrops. Even the confident crampons found it a little exposed on the way up.

Winter days are short and Stob Ban is far, so we headed down Bodach's south ridge, and found streaks of snow right down to the path.

Mamores ridgeline, towards Na Gruagaichean

Next day, sun still shining; Mamores still obstructing the road to Loch Linnhe. Alois, exhausted by so much sunny Scotland, took the bus to Ballachulish. Alone, I cramponed back to the ridge in a breeze stiff enough to be alarming. I'd started at dawn, so nobody else was around. The morning sky was not just blue, but blue-green, with an intensity normally got by improper use of photographic filters. This was like the Alps, except that, as Alois has pointed out, the view had lochs in, and the sub-zero sun couldn't turn the snow to midday slush. I took a long solitary pause on Mullach nan Coirean, simply being there. South across the Aonach Eagach, Bidean looked particularly splendid. But then, so did everything else.

There are various ways down Glen Nevis. The road is simply horrid, with spruce trees on the left and the dull side of Ben Nevis opposite. The forest track is slightly less horrid, no cars but even more spruce. I took the third way, on the wrong side of the river – and found Glen Nevis is a beautiful place. Backlit, you don't notice the grim spruce. The river chuckles over golden stones just loudly enough to drown out the cars on the other side. Birches make twiggy lacework against the light. It's all later in the book as Route 12.

I visited the Old Fort, but resisted the temptation to head onwards along the new Great Glen Way. It'd be a lot less Great than Ben Lui and the Buachaille Beag. After five days, I was fit for the Nevisport carbohydrate whammy – macaroni with chips – and their pictures of Alpine ridges failed to arouse the usual jealous stirrings.

Scotland's weather is unpredictable. So often, it leaves plans stymied and unfulfilled. We'll have to do that blizzard plod up the West Highland Way another year.

PART 1
The High Road and the Low

Arriving at the summit Beinn a' Chrulaiste (Route 11) with Buachaille Etive Mor behind

MILNGAVIE TO DRYMEN

The train out to Milngavie passes through groves of weedy sycamores, with an understorey of spike-topped fencing and ground cover of brambles and plastic litter. Shrieks of the electric railway combine with warnings on the loudspeakers: don't forget your luggage, passenger safety notices are displayed within the carriage. All this makes it quite clear why one needs to get out of Glasgow, on foot, and head north among the mountains.

It also makes it clear why, however logically sensible, one doesn't want to start from Glasgow city centre. The Kelvin and Allander walkways would make that project possible. But we don't need 19km (12 miles) of litter-strewn urban cycleways to remind us why we want to get northwards towards Fort William. And the start at Milngavie is surprisingly satisfying (even if the Dumbarton start, in Route 17, is even more so.)

WH WAY: MILNGAVIE TO DRYMEN

Distance	20km (12½ miles)
Approximate time	5hr
Not the WH Way	Route 1: Campsie Fells
	Route 17: Dumbarton Start

Milngavie is part of Glasgow. From the station you pass under a main road to cafés, and a chemist's shop, and a pedestrian precinct for those who like their pedestrianism tarmacked and lined with retail outlets. But under the wrought iron arch and down the steps, branches of trees replace branches of Next and Topshop, and over the following 13km or so (8 miles) you're going to cross just three metalled roads.

The paths through the Mugdock Country Park are helpfully signposted. Sometimes the WH Way runs with the river to its left, and sometimes up to the right of it past small outcrops of black basalt, and under birch and oak trees well draped with greybeard lichen – this showing how unpolluted the air is even so close to Glasgow.

Halfway through the bluebells, you'd fork right for the diversion over the Campsie Fells below. On the main path you pass Carbeth Loch, a shanty-town from the inter-war years, head briefly to the left along a road then back right on the path, and enjoy the sudden view along Strath Blane.

The path dodges around wooded Dumgoyach, an abrupt volcanic plug, and joins an old railway. This runs along an old aqueduct: Loch Lomond is out of sight ahead, but its waters are heard inside the metal pipe beside you. The final miles to Drymen are along the minor road through Gartcosh: a bit to be walked over briskly.

WH Way walkers approach Dumgoyne

ROUTE 1
Hill Option: the Campsie Fells

Start	Milngavie
Finish	Drymen
Distance	29km (18 miles)
Ascent	850m (2900ft)
Approximate time	9hr
Maximum altitude	578m Earl's Seat
Terrain	Grassy hill paths

The Cuillin: peat bog and black rock, jagged ridges and swirling mist, and even your trusty compass conspires against you. The Cairngorms: huge gravel plateaux, jammed up against sky, and after six hours of boring walking you fall over an enormous crag. So what are the distinctive risks and difficulties of Scotland's third C-named hill range? Well, in the Campsie Fells you might lie down in the squashy grass to admire the view of Loch Lomond, fall asleep, and be a little bit late for your tea…

Tea is the appropriate beverage. Tea served in an elegant cup, with a piece of buttery shortbread. For these are the couthie* Campsies, the polite hills, the pleased-to-meet-you hills. In later days comes the struggle with the scree slope, the flog across the heather. Here on the edge of Glasgow is smooth suburban grass, a pretty picture of Loch Lomond, and a wee nip of whisky at the end of the day. Really, nothing could be nicer.

Including the Campsies makes for a long first day to Drymen. Instead you could take a 7km (4-mile) evening walk, and stop for the first night away from the hurly-burly of the West Highland Way at Strathblane village. Strathblane and nearby Blanefield have shops, pubs and a takeaway café. From there over the Campsies to Drymen is a moderate day of 22.5km and 750m (14 miles and 2500ft) – about 7 hours.

*Couthie: snug, sociable, homely (Scots).

From Milngavie walk the WH Way for 2.5km, to where Allander Water is beside the path, with a golf course opposite. As the path bends slightly right, uphill away from the stream, turn off right, more steeply uphill, on a path signed for Mugdock Castle.

The path heads uphill, then with open field on its left passes through an artistic wall snitch with poetic slogans. It continues as a timber walkway through

Not the West Highland Way: A Mountain High Way

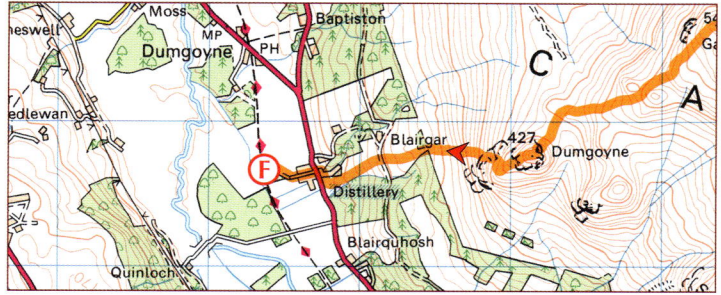

hilltop bog. Keep ahead across two wider paths to pass immediately to left of **Mugdock Castle** (a ruin, open to wander in).

The path descends to cross open bog, then re-enters trees and forks to reach a crossing track. Here turn right, signed for East and South Lodge Car Parks. The wide path runs to left of Mugdock Loch (not the same as Mugdock Reservoir further south). At the next junction keep ahead for East Car Park. Reaching it, turn right along a road very briefly to the edge of Mugdock Country Park, then turn sharp left, signed for Strathblane.

Follow the minor road north into the edge of **Strathblane**. The road dips to pass a pond on the right. At the next junction, the road plunges steeply into the village to reach a T-junction at the village green and small shop.

Turn right to the A81, and left to Kirkhouse Inn. Here turn right to take the A891 towards Campsie Glen. Here you could divert onto the railway path to right of the road for 1km. Pass a church on the left and its car park on the right. After 1km, look up left to glimpse a waterfall, way up in Ballagan Burn. To right of the road is the small steep volcanic plug Dunglass. The road passes the woods of **Ballagan House**.

At 1.2km from Strathblane, at the end of the wood on the left, go through a gate on the left and up onto open hill. Pass a fence corner on your right and slant up to the right to meet a grassy track. Follow this up left at first, then in zigzags.

Descending from Garloch Hill towards Dumgoyne

Route 1 – Hill Option: the Campsie Fells

After a gate, the track forks: take the right branch, soon forking right again on a faint path that joins the ridgeline fence that's the boundary between Stirling and East Dunbartonshire Councils. The grassy path left of the fence leads to the trig point on **Dumbreck**. The path and fence continue north, through a damp col and then a rather peaty one, to the trig point on **Earl's Seat**.

Take a path northwest, over a bent fence, to the top of the northern scarp. The path follows this edge southwest, as it rises to a viewpoint cairn, then dips and rises again to **Garloch Hill**. Then it wanders down to the col at the back of Dumgoyne.

The Campsies are made of volcanic basalt. It's the flat-topped lava flows, one on top of the other, that give these hills their grassy tops and sudden small crags. But Dumgoyne is the actual vent of one of the volcanoes. It's one of the most sudden and steep-sided hills in all Scotland. At the start I compared the Campsies somewhat mockingly with the Cuillin of Skye. Steep grass and a bit of basalt aren't at all the same as black bare rock. But in terms of pointiness at the top, Dumgoyne is up there with Sgurr nan Gillean and Am Basteir.

So while there's a bypass path on the right, it's worth taking the small, very steep, path that zigzags up ahead to the summit of **Dumgoyne**. The views may not be quite so stunning as on Sgurr nan Gillean but they're still pretty grand, and the grassy hollows are more tempting to rest among than Gillean's black ledges.

Take a path just south of west, down a grassy spur. As it steepens, avoid a steep and eroded direct descent to the right. Keep on down the spur path a bit further, until it turns sharp right, to contour across the steep northwestern face. It crosses the eroded straight-down path, then passes below some columnar basalt, to reach gentler slopes below.

Various paths descend westwards towards **Glengoyne Distillery**, converging on a stile. Across this, fork left down a dip in a field between two ash trees to another stile. The path runs down a final field to the roadside just south of the distillery.

Turn right to the distillery, and cross the road to a track between whisky warehouses, the distillery's parking area. Through a gate the track becomes a rough field track, bending right, then reaching the **WH Way**. Turn right – you've still got 10km to do to Drymen.

DRYMEN TO ROWARDENNAN

Conic Hill from south of Luss

This short stage finishes crossing the Lowland plain and arrives at Loch Lomond. It's the only section without a mountain alternative – unless we count 361m Conic Hill as a mountain.

Maybe we should. Conic offers a stiff steep climb, a sudden panorama, and a whole lot of rock on top. That stiff, steep climb is, however, a mere 50m above the WH Way path. This is scarcely enough to justify 'mountain alternative' status and a little yellow box with distances and times.

WH WAY: DRYMEN TO ROWARDENNAN

Distance   24km (15 miles)
Approximate time   7hr

DRYMEN TO ROWARDENNAN

After the rail-and-road travel of the previous section, today starts with something even less exciting: a wood-pulp plantation. Leave Drymen on the main A811 for a path on the left up into Garadhban Forest.

The forest track contours northwest, through a car park and past various side-tracks. Emerge into a patch of clear-fell, and the official Way's first view of Loch Lomond lies below the brushwood. Here I met two Germans encamped in what had been, before the trees fell, a clearing: a point marked on Harvey's strip map as a wild campsite. I was pleased to tell them that, since the Land Reform Act of 2003, the whole of Scotland is a wild campsite. A more recent bylaw now forbids wild camping along Loch Lomond from Conic Hill north to Ptarmigan Lodge at Rowardennan. For myself, I continued into the darkness to a comfortable heather bed on the slopes of Conic Hill.

After the gate onto open moorland, the path becomes surprisingly rough, and not even very distinct at first. It tends uphill then bends round left onto the end of Conic Hill.

SMALL HILL SIDE-TRIP: CONIC HILL

Conic is the final leaping-upwards of the Lowlands. It's a slice of pebbly conglomerate, tipped on edge to form a spiky spine right down to Balmaha. The hill could be (but isn't) nicknamed as Conic the Hedgehog.

Leave the WH Way as it starts to slant round onto the right-hand slope of the hill, to ascend grassy heather to the summit; or else from the WH Way's high point, a small path leads back sharp left up to a col and the summit just beyond.

The summit features in the hill list of Marilyns: although only 361m high, it has the required 150m of drop all around it. Most Marilyns have fine views, and Conic's is a panorama of Loch Lomond. Ahead and below, the hill spine continues as a line of islands across the loch. Conic Hill and its islands are taken as marking the boundary between Lowlands and Highlands. On a clear day, that line can be extended beyond Loch Lomond to the distant Isle of Arran, also split into Lowland and Highland halves.

Descend southwest to the first col. Here the path leads down to the right to rejoin the WH Way; but for the full Conic tonic, continue down the hill spine, enjoying the views and being disconcerted by the bare conglomerate rocks on the steeper descents. The water-smooth cobbles embedded in the rock are of pale quartzite and dark lava. They were washed by flash floods out of a mountain range to the north that no longer exists. The quartzite cobbles are particularly slippery.

After 1km, slant down to the right to rejoin the WH Way, just as it bends back to the left to slant through a grassy col in the spine ridge.

NOT THE WEST HIGHLAND WAY: A MOUNTAIN HIGH WAY

The descent to Balmaha is not the Way's longest one – that distinction goes to the descent from the Devil's Staircase to Kinlochleven (see page 89). But it is the second longest, and the steepest, and coming so early on is undoubtedly the toughest. Even those planning all the ambitious big-hill byways for later on may find this downhill section bringing their knees (as it were) to their knees.

After bypassing the summit, the wide WH Way path continues down just to right of Conic's summit ridge. It is muddy and sometimes on bare conglomerate (or 'puddingstone') rock. It passes down leftwards through a grassy col and then into woods. Cross Balmaha car park, whose visitor centre has a sculpture symbolising the Highland Line in just two large stones, one of the Lowland Old Red Sandstone and the other of Highland schist.

From the lane to Balmaha pier, the path climbs over Craigie Fort, a fine viewpoint. And now we're in the Highlands. Specifically we're on Loch Lomond side, as rampaged over by Rob Roy Macgregor. But the woodland paths are well laid, the wild wolves extinct. Nothing lurks among the oaks but a sudden glimpse of Loch Lomond; and even the plumpest and most affluent West Highland walker probably won't be molested by any cattle-reiving bandit. Reiving (Scots): snatching away, thieving, especially of livestock. The victim is 'bereived', and may well over the coming winter be dying of hunger.

North of Milarrochy's shingle bay the way runs sometimes alongside the small tarred road, but mostly just far enough in the woods to be out of earshot. The path rejoins the road for half a mile, to the large car park at Rowardennan Pier.

Loch Lomond from Conic Hill

ROWARDENNAN TO INVERSNAID

WH Way path beside Loch Lomond

Having just spent half a day wandering the wooded shore of Loch Lomond, today will consist of – wandering the wooded shore of Loch Lomond. The shore of Loch Lomond is delightful and it'd be a shame to miss it. On the other hand, perhaps we don't need quite so much of it as 30km or 20 miles. Especially when Ben Lomond, one of Scotland's best-loved mountains, looms over the loch.

There are two ways to do Ben Lomond. On good paths, there's a circuit returning to Rowardennan over the Ptarmigan. Or there's the wild country option, descending the untrodden north ridge and crossing some rough moorland to pick up a track down to the loch again at Cailness.

WH WAY: ROWARDENNAN TO INVERSNAID

Distance	11km (7 miles)
Approximate time	3hr
Not the WH Way	Route 2: Ben Lomond
	Route 3: Hill Crossing: Ben Lomond to Inversnaid

Not the West Highland Way: A Mountain High Way

On stormy days – or ones that are merely dreich and damp – the lochside is less demanding. Indeed, the lochside is just great as wind sweeps the branches overhead and waves rattle against the shoreline rocks. From Rowardennan car park follow the shoreline past a granite war memorial in the shape of a stone ring. Just beyond it there are some glacier scratches in the shoreline rocks. Then join the track of the WH Way.

After passing above Ptarmigan Lodge, the WH Way turns down left off the vehicle track. (Staying on the track is easy, but uninteresting and saves very little time against the well-made path below it.) The new and well-made path runs through the woods above the shore. In fact it allows you to re-enact the lochside journey of September 1716 made by Montrose's redcoats on their way to raid Rob Roy at Inversnaid. The redcoats did it from Drymen overnight, in a rainstorm; today's smooth path is more enjoyable. Especially for those not trying to cross it quickly.

After 4km the lower path passes Rowchoish bothy, and soon after that rejoins the track above. This track shrinks to a wide, well-made path, and descends to the shoreline at Cailness. Here the high line over Ben Lomond rejoins the WH Way.

The final 3km to Inversnaid is a ramble along the shoreline. The path is well made but not too well made, winding under oak trees and stepping over a boulder. There are glimpses across the loch to the Cobbler and the other Arrochar hills. Even on a dismal wet day there's shelter under the trees and the sound of waves along the shoreline, not to mention the warm Inversnaid Hotel just ahead. It's a delightful moment of the Way: and one quite different from the various mountain moments still to come.

ROUTE 2
Rowardennan Outing: Ben Lomond

Start/finish	Rowardennan pier car park
Distance	10.5km (6½ miles)
Ascent	1050m (3500ft)
Approximate time	5hr
Maximum altitude	974m Ben Lomond
Terrain	Wide, smooth path up; steep rough one to start the descent, then a small but comfortable one

Ben Lomond used to be Scotland's most ascended mountain. In recent years it has been overtaken by Ben Nevis – but Ben Lomond's better. It has lovely Loch Lomond views, and a gentler slope, and a little ridgeline along the top. Plus, it doesn't go on upwards for the grumble-inducing extra 370m.

My son when walking the West Highland Way attempted Ben Lomond by its more ambitious Ptarmigan route, and was turned back by strong winds. To avoid such disappointment, this excursion uses the busy and straightforward south ridge path for the ascent. The descent will be by that dramatic northwest ridge and the Ptarmigan. From the top of Ben Lomond you can assess the first few metres of this ridge, contemplate the wind speed and the slipperiness, and decide to return by the easier southern route.

Ascending the south ridge of Ben Lomond

NOT THE WEST HIGHLAND WAY: A MOUNTAIN HIGH WAY

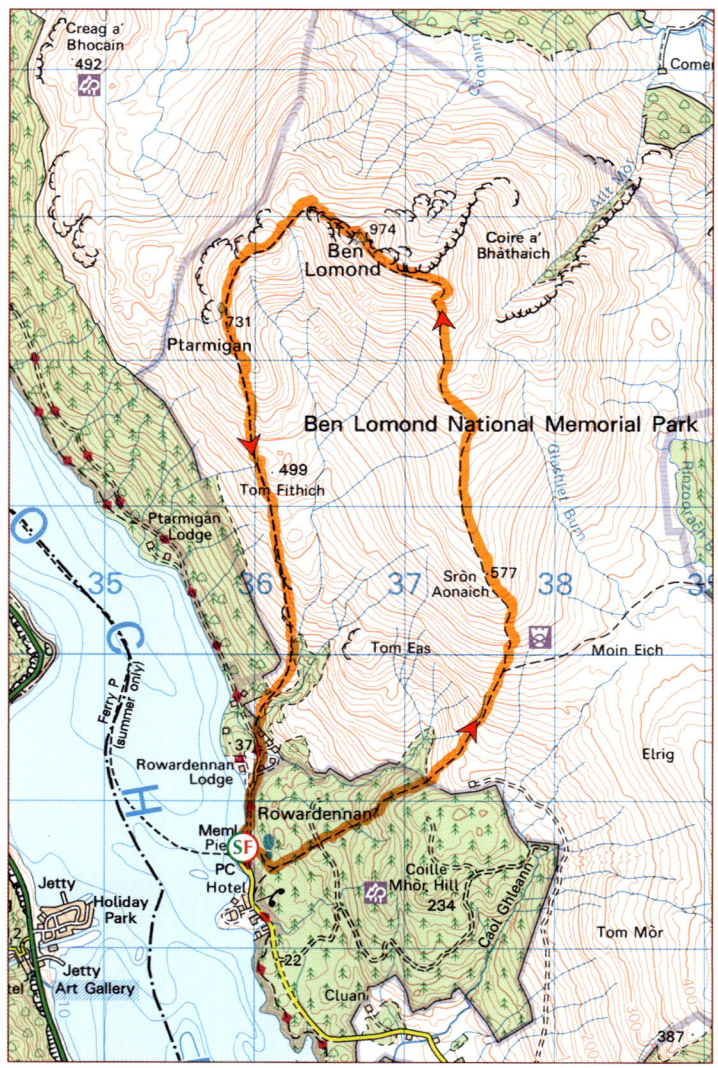

Route 2 – Rowardennan Outing: Ben Lomond

The ascent is on a wide, smooth path from the inland edge of the car park. Already by the 1860s this path was large enough to be marked on Ordnance Survey maps, and by the 1940s was an eroded eyesore – but has now been well rebuilt along a single line. The plantations that hemmed in the path have recently been clear-felled, so the views over Loch Lomond to the Lowlands are outstanding right from the start.

The path leaves the plantations at a gate, bends right onto the wide southern ridge, and goes up through another gate. Only at the final half-mile does the ground become mountainous, along a steep-sided and mildly rocky ridge.

From **Ben Lomond** summit trig point are views ahead of several dozen more large mountains including, on a clear day, Ben Nevis looking – from 71km (44 miles) away – depressingly distant.

The northwest ridge descends directly behind the trig point. The small gravelly path zigzags down among small rocky outcrops. The top section is as steep as any, so if conditions are too harsh you find that out straight away.

At 768m the ridge levels off. At this small shoulder, turn left, southwest. Route 3, the Ben Lomond crossing, turns down to the right here.

The fairly small but clear path winds along the **Ptarmigan ridge**, bending to the left as it gently descends. At about 600m altitude, the path eases down onto the right flank above Loch Lomond. It slants down to a fence gate, then passes below the Sput Ban waterfall. With the stream on its left, it heads directly downhill to join the track of the **WH Way**. Turn left for 800 metres, past the youth hostel, to the Rowardennan car park.

Ben Lomond seen from its Ptarmigan Ridge

Ptarmigan, Ben Lomond, and Rowardennan Youth Hostel from the old pier

Not the West Highland Way: A Mountain High Way

ROUTE 3
Hill Crossing: Ben Lomond to Inversnaid

Start	Rowardennan car park
Finish	Inversnaid
Distance	18km (11 miles)
Ascent	1200m (3900ft)
Approximate time	7hr
Maximum altitude	Ben Lomond 974m
Terrain	Smooth path up; small rocky ridge path down; grassy ridges and moorland, rough moorland, and a track

This route contrasts wild mountain ground that is part of a standard Munro-bagger's route with wild mountain ground that isn't. One of the widest and busiest paths in Scotland takes you up Ben Lomond. But on the other side is a small rugged ridge that's far less trodden, followed by a green ridge and some brown moorland that aren't trodden at all. On the complete crossing of Ben Lomond you'll discover that there are more interesting – there are *even* more interesting – routes than up to the summit from the nearest car park as quickly as possible.

Having led for most of a day high above Loch Lomond, the route takes a helpful track down to the shoreline. While all of Loch Lomond is lovable, the section you've just missed out is perhaps less lovable than some, while the 3km still to do are among the best.

On the northwest ridge of Ben Lomond, descending towards Ptarmigan Ridge

ROUTE 3 – HILL CROSSING: BEN LOMOND TO INVERSNAID

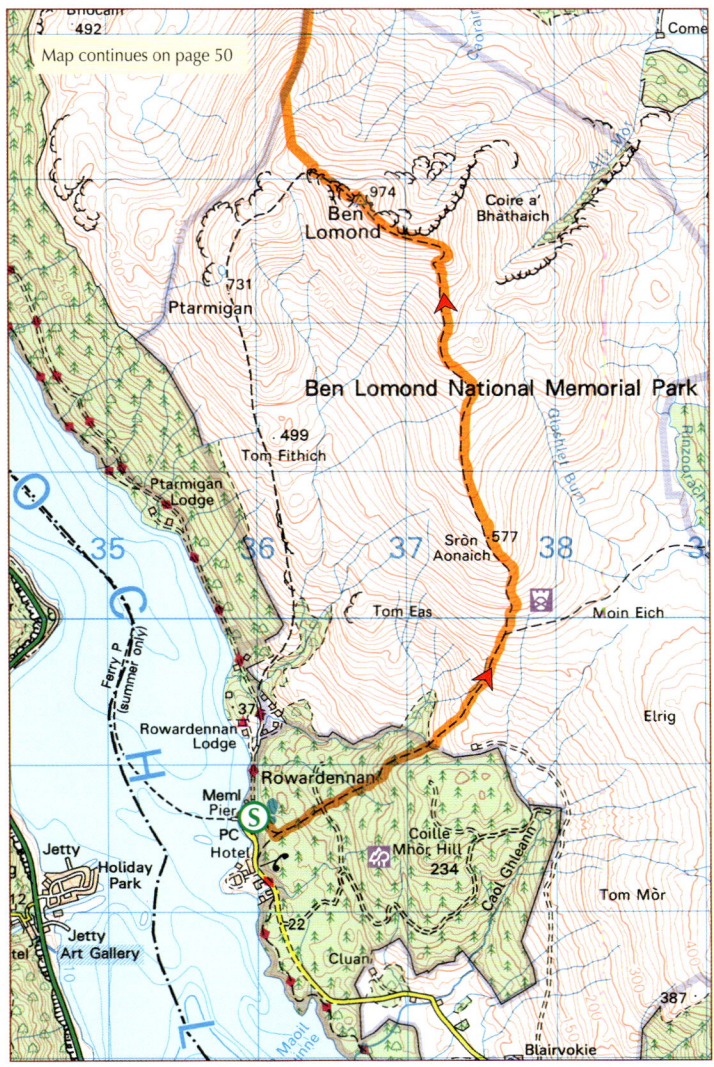

NOT THE WEST HIGHLAND WAY: A MOUNTAIN HIGH WAY

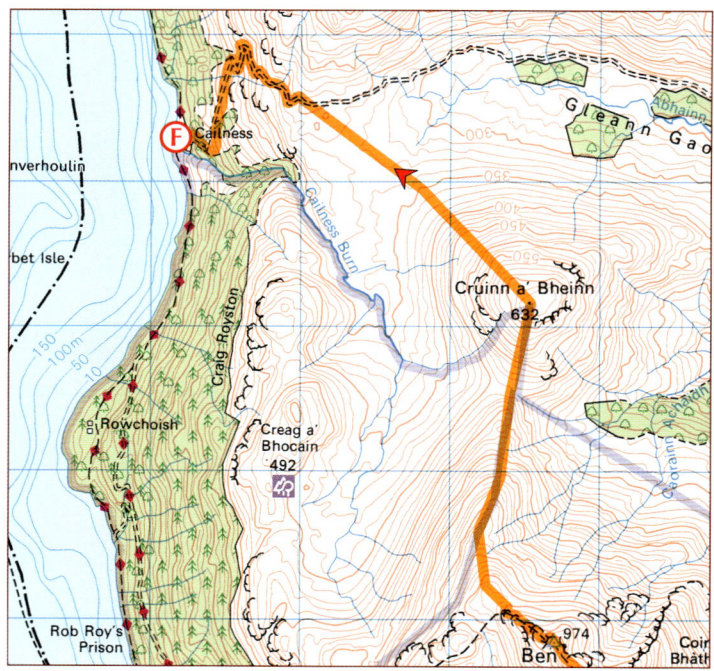

Use the previous route (Rowardennan outing: Ben Lomond) to **Ben Lomond** summit, and down the northwest ridge to the levelling at 768m. The pathless walking starts pleasantly, down the grassy ridge northwards. The going is briefly rough through the Bealach Cruinn a' Bheinn. A new deer fence crosses, but it's possible to squeeze between the wires so as to head up between small outcrops to **Cruinn a' Bheinn** itself. Cruinn a' Bheinn, pronounced Crinaven, means 'round hill'. As a Scottish hill of over 2000ft, it's classed as a Graham.

Cruinn a' Bheinn is ringed with small crags, but if you head carefully down northwest, following the remnants of an old fence line, there's a grassy break down. Follow the fence onwards into tussocky rough moorland. Cross this across its highest point. As the ground rises slightly, you meet a firm stony track. This leads down to the left in steep zigzags to **Cailness** cottage. Just below, the WH Way path runs along the shoreline.

Turn right for 3km to Inversnaid.

INVERSNAID TO INVERARNAN

The shoreline walk continues northwards, always pleasant and in places rather rough. Indeed, the 4.5km north of Inversnaid are the most rugged part of the WH Way – although in terms of the mountain deviations in this book, that's still only moderate ruggedness.

Overhead, the higher route along pathless Beinn a' Choin is also rather rough. So either way you get at least a feeling of what this country was like in the time of Rob Roy before the coming of the roads. For full authenticity you'd need to have soft deerskin moccasins, non-waterproof clothing, some redcoats in pursuit and the midges flying in underneath your kilt.

WH WAY: INVERSNAID TO INVERARNAN

Distance	10km (6 miles)
Approximate time	2.5hr
Not the WH Way	Route 4: Hill Crossing: Beinn a' Choin
	Route 5: Inverarnan Outing: Beinn Chabhair

North from Inversnaid, the lochside track soon diminishes to a wide path. After 500 metres from the hotel, an RSPB trail turns up right for a brief steep excursion into the trees, the main path continuing more easily at the same level. Soon

Doune and Doune Byre bothy, with distant view of Ben Lui

NOT THE WEST HIGHLAND WAY: A MOUNTAIN HIGH WAY

after this, however, the main path itself becomes rugged as it passes below a crag and descends steeply to where a sign points back left for **Rob Roy's Cave**. It's worth spending half an hour exploring the tumble of boulders where wild goats now sleep in the former bed of the brigand. The main path continues above the shoreline, still rugged and narrow. It passes through a clearing with the ruins of Pollochro, then crosses a meadow and heads uphill in a shallow valley. After 500 metres it descends, to pass **Doune Byre** bothy.

The path gradually drops to the shore, with views across to Ben Vorlich. It climbs away from the shore again, and a side-path leads down to the pier for the Ardlui ferry. The main path passes above the head of the loch, into the col behind Cnap Mor, the 'big hummock'.

> ### Small hill side-trip: Cnap Mor
> The rugged little summit itself is another minor side-trip: ten minutes' rough walking from the high point of the WH Way. There's no path and no way is better than any other. The hill corner is a fine viewpoint along Loch Lomond and is where, on my late-March walk up the Way, I lay in the grass and watched whooper swans migrating north for Iceland.

The path descends gradually through woods, passing above Inverarnan Inn (Drover's Inn) on the other side of the river. Then it descends, and crosses the edge of a water meadow to a footbridge into **Beinglas campsite**.

For **Inverarnan**, turn down left; the stream bank leads to left of the campsite to River Falloch. Follow the river up to cross the campsite's access bridge. A path leads to the left, alongside the A82, to the Drover's Inn. Meanwhile the **WH Way** will continue to right of the campsite along the slope foot.

North ridge of Beinn a' Choin, looking back along Loch Lomond

ROUTE 4
Hill Crossing: Beinn a' Choin

Start	Inversnaid Hotel
Finish	Inverarnan (Beinglas campsite)
Distance	14km (9 miles)
Ascent	1000m (3300ft)
Approximate time	6hr
Maximum altitude	Beinn a' Choin 770m
Terrain	Pathless grassy hill

Beinn a' Choin is the Hill of the Dog, but people will enjoy it too. It forms a long, rambling ridgeline above Loch Lomond. At 770m it is 200m lower than Ben Lomond, which makes it 200m easier, no?

Well, no. Because Beinn a' Choin falls short of the 914m mark that would make it a Munro, almost nobody bothers to go. There is no company on the hill, no noise or litter, but more importantly, no path. The untrodden grass is short to walk over, but it's surprising how much difference it makes having to choose your route every step of the way. Go over this hump, or try to circumvent it? Does that reddish patch mean shorter grass to walk on, or is it possibly a bog? And that's assuming you get it roughly right. Get it wrong, and you're lost.

The only way the Corbetts are smaller is the minor matter of size.

Note, too, that the glacier has done its job well here, if we take the job of a glacier as being to gouge. The slope above Loch Lomond is steep and craggy, all the way. There's no easy escape back to the West Highland Way below.

But that same steep edge gives great views up and down the water. And who's going to get lost anyway? There is, as it happens, a dead fence remnant all the way along. Well, almost all the way…

From **Inversnaid Hotel** return across the footbridge above the waterfall, and at once take a path turning up to the left. It climbs among trees, with a branch path on the right that would lead you to the Rob Roy Viewpoint above the loch. But the main path continues to reach a small car park.

Turn down the access track to cross Arklet Water and join a minor road. Follow this up to the right to **Garrison of Inversnaid**. The garrison here was built

ROUTE 4 – HILL CROSSING: BEINN A' CHOIN

to restrain Rob Roy, but Rob burnt it down, his son burnt it again, and what little remains is incorporated into the farm walls.

Pass through the car park here onto open hill, and head up rough grass. Slant around to the right to join a fence, leading uphill onto **Stob an Fhainne**. A grassy ridge with a very small path leads down northwards. Cross a grassy col and make your way up to **Beinn a' Choin**, its summit protected by a tiny crag.

The rambling and uncertain ridgeline northwards would be tricky to follow in mist, but for the fence that runs along it. Follow this north at first, then bending northwest over **Maol an Fhithich**. Beinn a' Choin is 'hill of the dog'; Maol an Fhithich is 'hump of the raven'.

The guiding fence turns north, to pass above Lochan Dubh and over **Stob nan Eighrach**. As it bends northeast, leave it to pass to right of Lochan nam Muc. Keep north across bumpy moorland onto the slight rise of **Cruach**. From here a grassy ridgeline leads down west of north. After passing under power lines, choose the easiest ground you can find to the Ben Glas Burn which crosses ahead. On the burn's further bank is a peaty path. This follows the burn downstream, past Beinglas Falls, to meet the WH Way at **Beinglas campsite**.

For **Inverarnan** go straight across the WH Way path, and turn right at River Falloch to the campsite entrance.

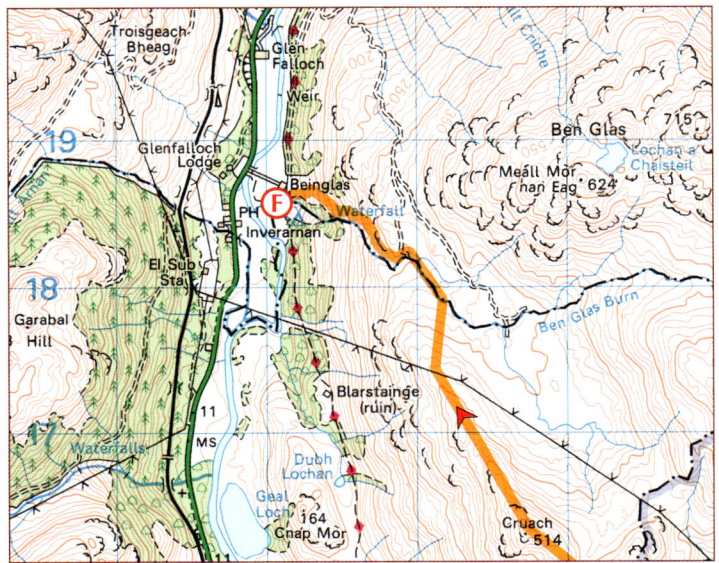

Not the West Highland Way: A Mountain High Way

ROUTE 5
Inverarnan Outing: Beinn Chabhair

Start/finish	Beinglas campsite, Inverarnan
Distance	15.5km (9½ miles)
Ascent	1350m (4500ft)
Approximate time	7hr
Maximum altitude	Beinn Chabhair 933m
Terrain	Rough paths, then pathless grassy hill ground

Beinn Chabhair is considered as a very minor Munro. Up it – down it the same way – and forget it. I think it deserves a little more attention. Above the waterfall use the valley path for the ascent, but divert onto a wilder spur of the hill. And to come down again ramble along the ridgeline to the Lochan of the Castle. It's a spot as romantic as its name, where your only chance of being overlooked while bathing alfresco is if someone on Ben Lui, 10km away across the glen, happens to have a pair of powerful binoculars.

The WH Way enters **Beinglas campsite** at a shelter signboard. From here a small path sets off uphill, starting with a stile behind some wigwam huts. It visits a corner above Beinglas waterfalls, then zigzags away to the left, before eventually rejoining the stream in the gentler hanging valley above.

Beinn Chabhair's northwest ridge, to Lochan a' Chaisteil

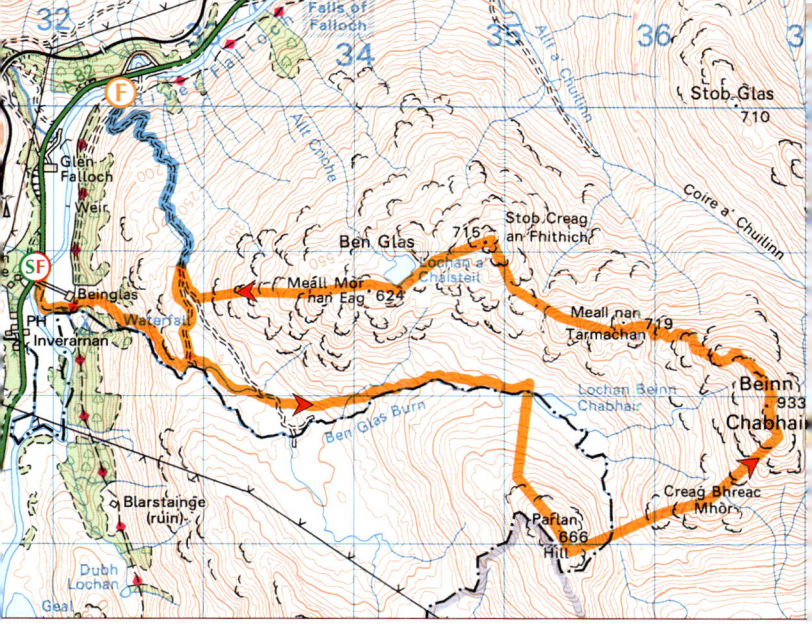

The path follows the stream to the outflow of Lochan Beinn Chabhair. Cross the stream on the right, and make a way over **Parlan Hill** to the col behind it. From here, a complicated-looking ridge leads up eastwards towards Beinn Chabhair. Outcrops blocking the direct line can be bypassed on the left, but rejoin the main ridgeline above. After a levelling, head up northeast on grass, weaving among outcrops, to reach the summit cairn of **Beinn Chabhair**.

A wide path leads onwards, down the shapely northwest ridge. After weaving among the knolls of **Meall nan Tarmachan** that path heads down left towards Lochan Beinn Chabhair. That's the quicker way back. But if you're feeling lively, continue northwest along the knolly ridgeline. **Stob Creag an Fhithich** ahead rises like a grassed-up Matterhorn. It's closer, smaller, and more pregnable than it looks.

From Stob Creag an Fhithich descend to Lochan a' Chaisteil. Linger along its shores, then pass over the slight rise beyond, named as Meall Mor nan Eag. Keep on down westwards, on a slope that's basically gentle but is interrupted by small crags. At 330m the ground levels and becomes rougher. Here a rough track runs across.

If you turn right here, it will lead you down to the **WH Way** continuing northwards. Or, to return to **Beinglas campsite**, take the path to the left, soon rejoining the upward path beside Beinglas Burn.

INVERARNAN TO TYNDRUM

Beinn a' Chaisteal from the WH Way

From the head of Loch Lomond right through to Rannoch Moor there's one obvious way north. It's the way the Rannoch glacier took coming south, reaching the Lowlands with enough power still to gouge out the trough of Loch Lomond. It's the way north of the old military road now the WH Way, and of the modern A82, and the railway, and even a set of high-voltage power pylons.

The glacier valley is just about big enough for all of them. Along the old military road, the thrice-daily clatter of the train to Fort William will hardly disturb you, and the A82 on the other side is almost out of earshot. With any luck, low cloud will waft romantically among the pylons.

But when the sunlight sparkles on the car roofs, and the pylons stand proud against a blue sky, you might prefer to get up out of it all. The passage between the peaks of Ben Lui is real mountain ground, but with what should be the boggy bit at the beginning obliterated by a handy hydro-board track. It's a stiff climb to the 700m mark – and an even stiffer one if the spirit moves you to the summit of Ben Lui alongside. Descend empty Glen Cononish, past some ancient pines: and the WH Way, and the railway, and that old A82 can come as quite a surprise.

That's the high way through to Tyndrum. But for those who like a mix of civilisation with their wilderness, there's an option to take the WH Way and its glacier valley, but split into two bits. Take a break at Crianlarich for a hill experience that's less big than Ben Lui, with a helpful hillwalkers' path – but that still gives two Munros and a bit of the best of the Southern Highlands.

WH WAY: INVERARNAN TO TYNDRUM

Distance	30km (19 miles)
Approximate time	8hr
Not the WH Way	Route 6: Hill Crossing: Ben Lui (high pass or summit)
	Route 7: Crianlarich Outing: An Caisteal and Beinn a' Chroin

Beyond **Beinglas campsite**, the WH Way continues along the right (east) flank around the first curve of Glen Falloch, following a smooth track through woods. After 1.5km it forks up right on a good path, which soon runs just above River Falloch.

At **Derrydaroch Farm** it crosses the river. At once it turns off right on a roughish path upstream. After 1.5km, this bends uphill to a low creep under the railway, and then a metal culvert under the A82. This is the first crossing of this main road that's been in earshot all the way up Loch Lomond, and with which the WH Way will now become more intimately entwined.

The path slants uphill to become a contouring track. After 1km at a junction, take the uphill track. The downhill track leads to the A82 just south of the start of the mountain circuit over An Caisteal and Beinn a' Chroin (Route 7).

The main WH Way turns up left; on this short ascent there are reddish-brown garnets in the track stones. Soon the track levels along the valley's western side, above the pylons and almost unaware of the main road below. It passes above **Keilator Farm** to reach the edge of plantations.

Here the path downhill is for **Crianlarich**. Meanwhile, the WH Way continues through the plantations, then descends beside a stream to pass under the railway and recross the A82 to a bridge over **River Fillan**.

Once across the long bridge, a riverside path on the left is an option in lambing time for those with dogs, but the main WH Way is ahead along the access track to Kirkton Farm. Before the buildings, take a track to the left, past the ruins of St Fillan's Chapel, and on to **Auchtertyre**. Pass the campsite, wigwams and small shop, then turn left down the driveway.

NOT THE WEST HIGHLAND WAY: A MOUNTAIN HIGH WAY

Ben More and Stob Binnein from Auchtertyre

Before the A82, a stile on the left is a short side-path to visit St Fillan's healing pool. Just beyond, ease left under the bridge of the A82, then join a wide path alongside River Fillan. With Dalrigh on your right, join a track running left across a bridge. In just 300 metres turn right at a signpost, leaving the track on a well-made path.

The path continues through young pine and across bare ground poisoned by a former lead smelter. It rambles under tall pines to the edge of Tyndrum. Turn right for the village centre, or follow the WH Way markers ahead to pass the By the Way Hostel.

ROUTE 6
Hill Crossing: Ben Lui

Start	Inverarnan
Finish	Tyndrum
Distance	22km (13½ miles) *(High line over Ben Lui: 23.5km (14½ miles))*
Ascent	750m (2500ft) *(1200m (4000ft))*
Approximate time	7hr *(8hr)*
Maximum altitude	Ben Lui pass 690m *(Ben Lui 1130m)*
Terrain	Smooth paths to forest top, then pathless hill and rough path

When people first went into mountains, they weren't after any summits: they were just looking for the least difficult way through. The crossing of a high pass still makes a satisfying hill day. As you cross Gleann nan Caorann, the only way forward is blocked by the high ridgeline of Ben Lui. A track takes you most of the way up; you hurry through the windswept moorland gap, cloud racing overhead and rain beating sideways. The first descent is steep and rather awkward. But once down the sheltered V-slot of the stream, with its small path, it leads intimately outwards to the new glen on the other side.

On the other hand, if the cloud isn't racing overhead and the rain happens to be away, you could come over all contemporary and bag that summit above. Ben Lui is the finest hill in the Southern Highlands. And for those prepared to lug up the luggage, its high northern corrie is one of the compelling camps.

From **Inverarnan** walk north along the A82 (which is quite busy, so this is best done at dawn). After 1.5km – and just before the crossing of Dubh Eas sidestream – turn left through a gate and up a steep tarred lane. It passes over the railway and zigzags up to a T-junction at 250m on **Troisgeach Bheag**. Before dawn you don't see the power pylons, and just get the special mauve and grey view back along Loch Lomond.

At the track 'T' turn right, to contour into **Gleann nan Caorann**. The track follows a half-buried aqueduct pipe. After 4km, turn down right on a track that follows a huge metal pipe down to the valley floor and up the slope beyond. Near the top of the pipeline a track turns off right over a bridge, to continue uphill to the 570m contour on the flank of Ben Oss.

Route 6 – Hill Crossing: Ben Lui

At this level the heather moorland gives way to grassy slopes. The track as such ends here, although wheelmarks in the grass continue up in the same direction. The top of the actual track is marked by a small wooden box for sheep feed. Here turn off left, across the stream. Head northwest, around the hill and gradually uphill, into the wide col between **Ben Lui** and **Ben Oss**. The high line over Ben Lui summit turns up left here.

Cross the wide, knolly col at its lowest point, just east of a small pool. Descend northeast on a small path found immediately west of a pointy knoll (GPS users in mist: program in NN 2745 2465). This gives a comfortably grassy descent, if steep. As the slope eases into **Coire Laoigh** head down to left of the stream, finding a small but pleasant path. It runs right out along the valley below.

As the valley opens out, the river dips to the right past two grassy knolls. Here bear up left across pathless moorland. A path reforms alongside (to left of) a stream as you follow it up to a ford where a track starts on the right. The high line over Ben Lui rejoins the main route here.

Follow the track out along **Glen Cononish**, passing above **Cononish Farm**. After 1.5km beside the river, a track branches left into the plantations. That track is the quicker way, passing between the trees to Tyndrum lower station (saves 1km). The more enjoyable way is ahead, along the open valley by the river, with ancient pinewoods over on your right, to pass under the railway. In another 400 metres, turn off left on the path of the WH Way.

Ben Lui, seen from An Chaisteal. Route 6 crosses the group from front left to back right

NOT THE WEST HIGHLAND WAY: A MOUNTAIN HIGH WAY

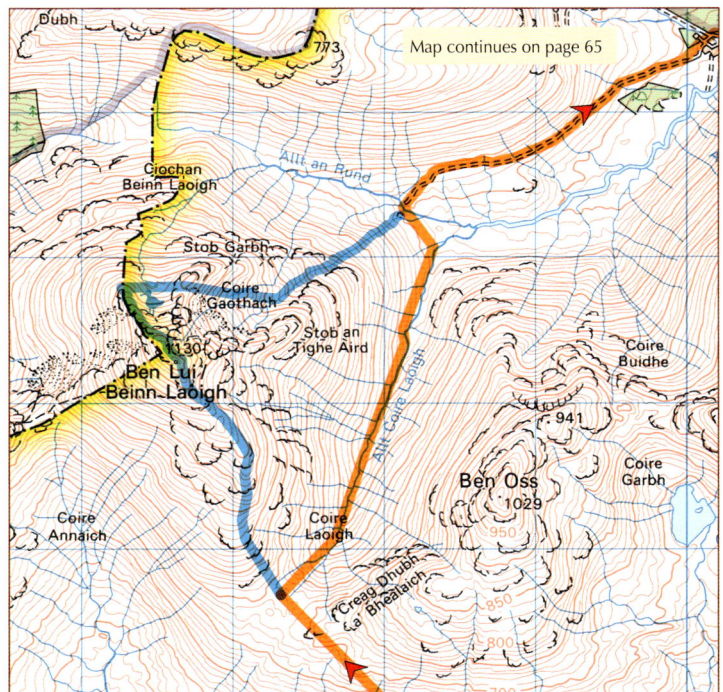

High line over Ben Lui summit

Follow the main route to the col between **Ben Lui** and **Ben Oss**.

Turn left (northwest) up a broad slope. It gradually narrows into a rounded ridge, with a path. This heads up north, then northwest, to **Ben Lui**'s summit cairn.

Continue ahead, down around the corrie rim as it bends right, up to the northwest summit. It's almost as airy as the main one. Continue down ahead for about 30 metres, to where a steep spur down to the right is the northeast ridge – but the better way bends left, down the pathed northwest ridge. As you descend, directly ahead is Ben Cruachan.

On the way down, the ridge path has a scrambling moment, on clean rock and not exposed. At 950m, the ridge becomes grassy and less steep. Here turn down right into **Coire an Lochain** with its pools (unnamed on Landranger but sporting a blue duck). As a campsite this is good in every way except in windy

Ben Lui from Ben Oss. Coire Gaothach is on the right

weather. Even with winds from the south it's breezy because of the way Ben Lui sticks up into the airstream (see photographs on pages 115 and 123).

Cross the corrie rim below the pools, and ease up right to a col, with a small cairn, on Ben Lui's northwest ridge. A path arrives here from up on the right. This path continues down ahead in zigzags towards **Coire Gaothach**, bending left as it approaches the corrie floor. Down in the corrie, it joins a path heading straight down to left of the main stream.

Once out of the corrie the path steepens. Towards the slope foot it slants down to the left, away from the main stream. It passes just above a sheepfold to reach a smaller stream. On the other side of this is the start of the track running out along **Glen Cononish**.

Follow the track out to the **WH Way** as on the main route.

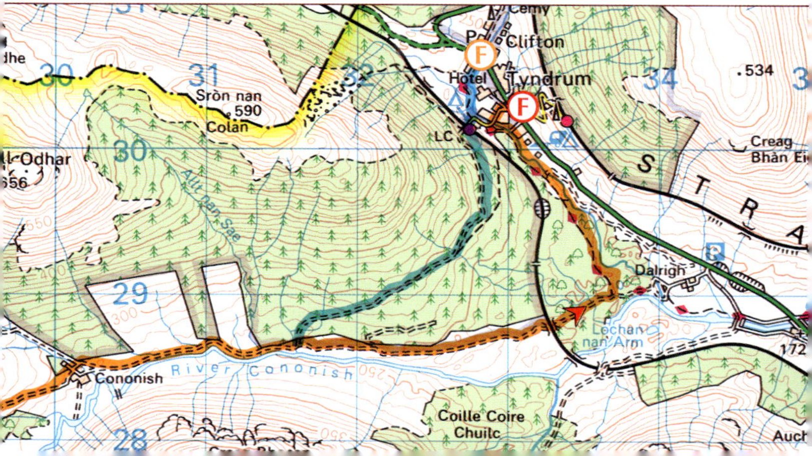

Not the West Highland Way: A Mountain High Way

ROUTE 7
Crianlarich Outing: An Caisteal and Beinn a' Chroin

Start/finish	Crianlarich
Distance	21.5km (13½ miles)
Ascent	1250m (4200ft)
Approximate time	8hr
Maximum altitude	An Caisteal 995m
Terrain	Small, rough hill paths

The obvious excursion from Crianlarich is Ben More. It's the highest hill in Lomond-Trossachs National Park, the second highest in the former Perthshire. Your pride at standing on the second-highest point of Perthshire will surely obliterate the memory of the intolerably long and steep grassy slope you slogged up to get there. (Sadly, though, there's still that intolerably long slope to slog back down again.)

So here's the less-obvious excursion. It offers two Munro summits, neither of them especially celebrated, even if Beinn a' Chroin does mean 'summit of some danger'. But the Chroin and the Castle offer ridgelines of grass and swirly schist rock, with a winding peaty path. The way is interesting without being particularly tricky. The two offer ordinary, enjoyable walking in a style typical of the Southern Highlands.

Shame about the soggy return along Glen Earb.

From Crianlarich Station the hill foot lay-by is a 2km walk back along the A82. Nicer, but longer, is to backtrack along the WH Way to the track junction southwest of **Keilator**. Turn down to the A82 and return towards Crianlarich for 400 metres (the distance given above includes the longer way by the WH Way path). This longer, but pleasanter, alternative is shown in blue on the accompanying map. One good plan is to avoid backtracking at all by incorporating this into a trail day from Inverarnan to Crianlarich (including the hill circuit, 26.5km [16½ miles] and 1400m [4700ft], about 9.5hr).

The hill path starts at a lay-by (section of former road) south of the A82 opposite the corner of plantations. A stile out of the lay-by leads onto a field path with wet bits – although returning at the end of the day, it'll seem (by contrast) like a very firm dry path.

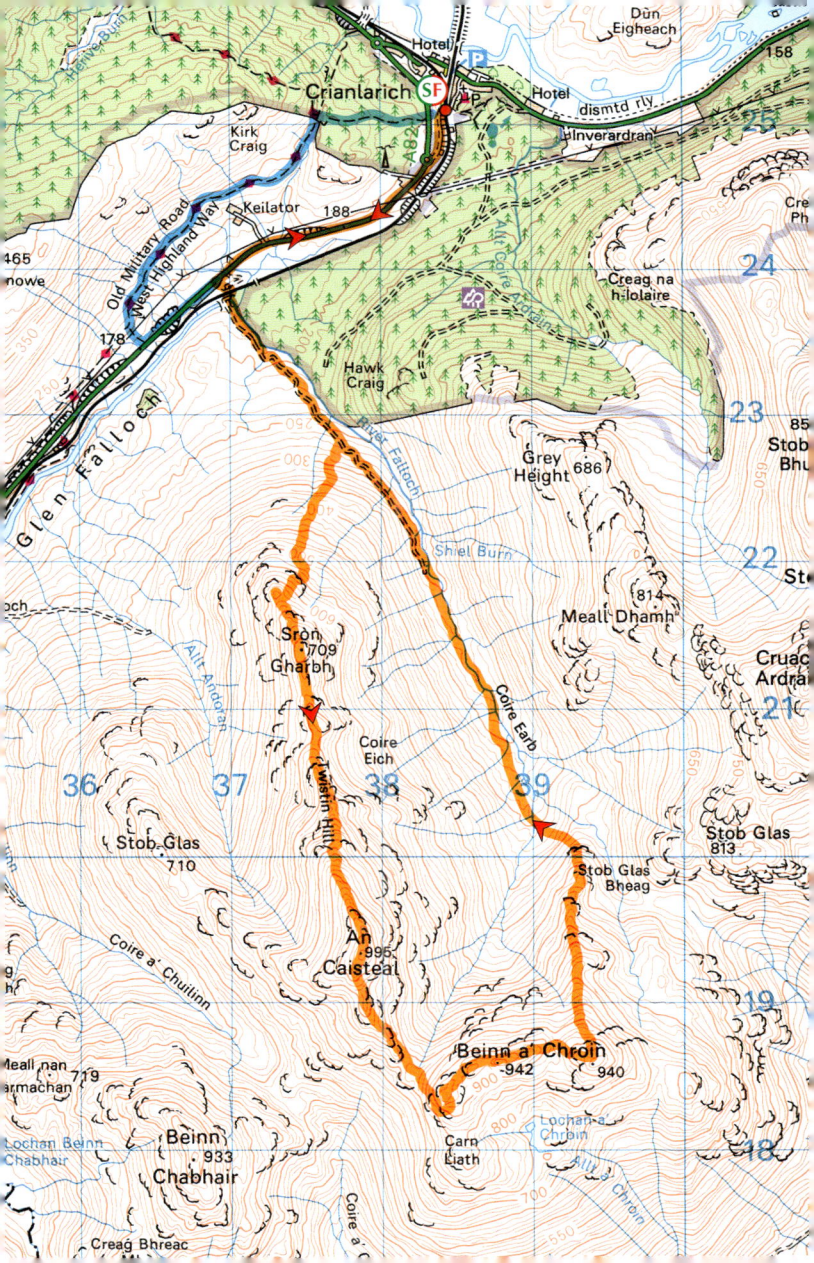

Descending An Caisteal's south ridge with Ben Lomond on the skyline

The path joins a track to a bridge under the railway and then another over River Falloch. Follow the track past the felled plantations to a gate. Here a rough path turns up right into bog; it may be better to continue 150 metres to where the track levels, and head from there through grass and rushes, right up onto **Sron Gharbh**.

Here a path runs south along the ridgeline, dodging around occasional outcrops. The enjoyable ridge is called Twistin Hill. A slight scramble crosses a landslip notch in the ridge, almost a crevasse. The 'castle' at 950m isn't the summit but gives the hill its name. It can be scrambled along its crest, or a path runs left along the foot of the rocks. The path continues to **An Caisteal** summit, which has three cairns.

Descend the path south then southeast on a ridge that's even more knolly than Twistin Hill was. If the path leads to the top of down-scramble groove with sloping holds, you can turn up right, across the ridgeline, and find a path below a crag round to the foot of the obstacle. The path then descends steeply, slanting right, to a wide col Bealach Buidhe.

The path across the col could be lost in mist as it splits apart: a compass bearing (147° magnetic) is useful. Head to the right-hand end of the obstructing crag line, and slant up to the right in a grassy gully on a clear path. The path then contours right, among western crags, and zigzags up to a scrambling move. The short move is steep and somewhat exposed, but with good holds.

ROUTE 7 – CRIANLARICH OUTING: AN CAISTEAL AND BEINN A' CHROIN

Emerge at a small cairn to a grass plateau, and another short rise east to pass through a notch onto the summit plateau of **Beinn a' Chroin**. A small path heads east, to the west summit (938m), with a distinctive boulder to its right. The true top is on bare rock beside the cairn.

Continue over the true summit (942m), which has its cairn on bare rock with a short vertical step to reach it. The path then dips with a scramble move, to pass just down to left of a col. It then climbs to the Beinn a' Chroin's eastern top, once taken to be the summit but now realised to be 2m too low.

Just below this east top the path divides. Turn up right for a few metres to the summit, then return and take the path heading down roughly north. Ill-defined at first, it soon becomes clear and a bit eroded as it descends the well-defined north ridge. Near its foot the ridge becomes lumpy and the path winds from side to side before reaching the grassland of the valley floor.

Here the path bends left, northwest, passing a dead tree to reach a stream crossing above a confluence. It crosses the second stream and heads north, down-valley, to left of **River Falloch**. It is mostly clear, with many boggy bits. After about 2.5km you reach the start of the valley track, and follow it ahead to rejoin the outward route to the A82 lay-by.

If you want to reach **Crianlarich** by the shorter road route, the A82 is busy and noisy but has a reasonable grass verge to walk on.

Beinn a' Chroin from the north

Not the West Highland Way: A Mountain High Way

TYNDRUM TO INVERORAN

The great northward valley continues, with the West Highland Way on its old military road intertwining with the West Highland Railway and today's A82 trunk road. Above them all stands the imposing cone of Beinn Dorain. The mountain alternative winds in around the back, to emerge suddenly at a point almost 900m above the WH Way and the railway.

WH WAY: TYNDRUM TO INVERORAN

Distance	15km (9½ miles)
Approximate time	4hr
Not the WH Way	Route 8: Hill Crossing: the back of Beinn Dorain
	Route 9: Inveroran Outing: Beinn Inverveigh and Meall Tairbh

The WH Way leaves **Tyndrum** by the road bridge at its north end, and turns up right past Brodie's Mini-Mart on the old road out of the village. At the slope-top

Beinn Dorain and Auch Gleann

the track approaches the A82 but then bends right, over the railway, and runs just above it. The tall, steep cone of Beinn Odhar stands above the trail. It's an impressive landmark – at least until you top the pass and see the taller, steeper and even more conical Beinn Dorain rising behind it.

After 1km, fork right on a path that wanders a little further up the slope of Beinn Odhar before dropping under the railway through a cattle creep and rejoining the track.

The track runs gently downhill towards **Auch Farm** with Beinn Dorain rising above it. At cross tracks, the Auch Gleann runs up to the right, under the left-hand of the two rail viaducts, and is the start of the diversion over Beinn Dorain. But the WH Way keeps ahead to cross the wide stream (Allt Kinglass).

The WH Way continues along the old military road, running just below the railway and then just above it, to reach the station at **Bridge of Orchy**. Cross the main road past Bridge of Orchy Hotel, and then cross the bridge itself, over River Orchy, just below.

After Bridge of Orchy, the WH Way parts from its younger offspring the A82. With that noisy brat finally away on its own path through life, we can return to the older way, the hill way. As the lane bends right just after the bridge, take the waymarked WH path opposite the bridge. It slants up to the right, soon entering plantations. At the top of the forest it takes a zigzag back left, then contours pleasantly to a cairn at its high point, **Mam Carraigh**. This cairn on its hill ridge above Loch Tulla gives the illusion of remoteness, although the comfortable **Inveroran Hotel** is only a quarter-hour down the trail.

Not the West Highland Way: A Mountain High Way

ROUTE 8

Hill Crossing: the back of Beinn Dorain

Start	Tyndrum
Finish	Bridge of Orchy
Distance	24.5km (15½ miles)
Ascent	1300m (4400ft)
Approximate time	9hr
Maximum altitude	Beinn Dorain 1076m
Terrain	Tracks, pathless grassy hill, hill paths, rough steep path for descent

The standard route up Beinn Dorain and its neighbour Beinn an Dothaidh is almost a parody of hill-bagging. March up the steep stony path to the col. Bag to the right: Beinn Dorain. Bag to the left: Dothaidh. March back down the steep stony path. If the two Munros are an unpleasant chore, this is the quickest way to get them done. If the two Munros are grouse, well done, you just shot them out of the sky.

Dorain deserves better. Dorain is no dead bird, but a fine hill celebrated in 554 lines of Gaelic poetry by Duncan Ban MacIntyre. A wander up the Auch Gleann takes you past the remains of Duncan Ban's actual home. It also takes you away from the road and railway, between green slopes with a quiet river running between.

After the long, rambling, back way in, you arrive suddenly on Dorain's summit ridge and the view westwards to the massed hills of the Black Mount. The summit ridge is appreciated all the more for not having slogged up that bad path from Bridge of Orchy.

Once at the col above Coire an Dothaidh, you stop and examine your ethics. Beinn an Dothaidh, we're afraid, will now be that standard baggers' out and back. But at least it postpones the grim descent of the baggers' path down to Bridge of Orchy.

From the WH Way just before the bridge over **Allt Kinglass**, turn right up the track into Auch Gleann. The track runs to the right of the river, forking left to pass under the left-hand of the two big viaducts. Once in the Auch Gleann, the track fords the river half a dozen times. After 4km, it passes farm sheds: this is a barn conversion

Route 8 – Hill Crossing: the back of Beinn Dorain

in reverse, as the lower walls of the eastern half are the cottage **Ais an t-Sithean**. This was the home of Duncan Ban MacIntyre, the poet of Beinn Dorain. Sithean are the fairies, and Ais an t-Sithean is possibly the Fairy Ferry.

In 1km more take a side-track on the left – the main track ahead is the baggers' standard route for the boring Munro Beinn Mhanach. Our side-track slants

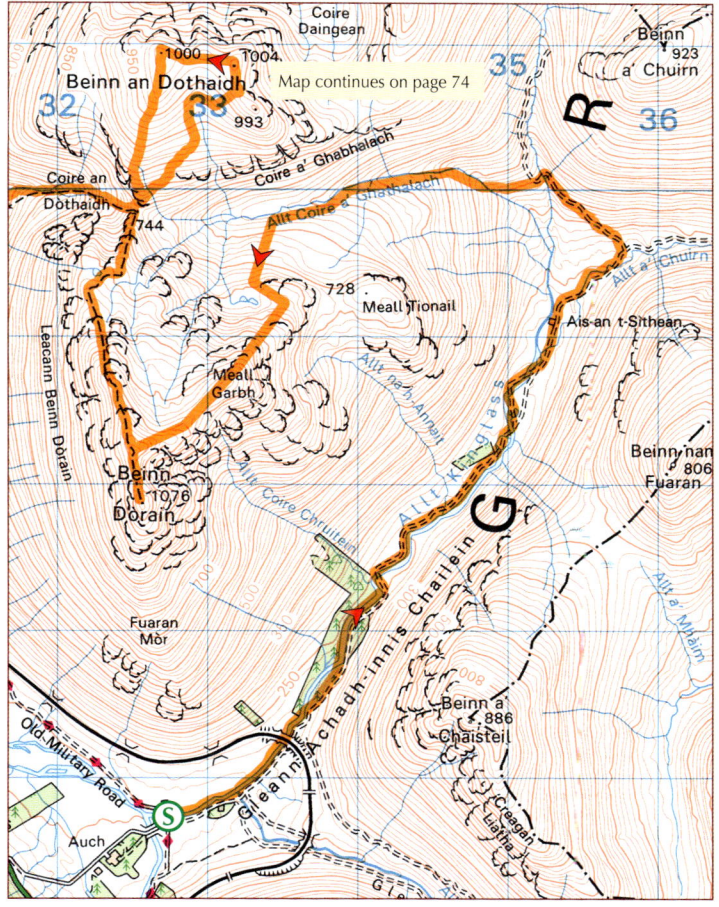

NOT THE WEST HIGHLAND WAY: A MOUNTAIN HIGH WAY

Up Auch Gleann to reach the back of Beinn Dorain

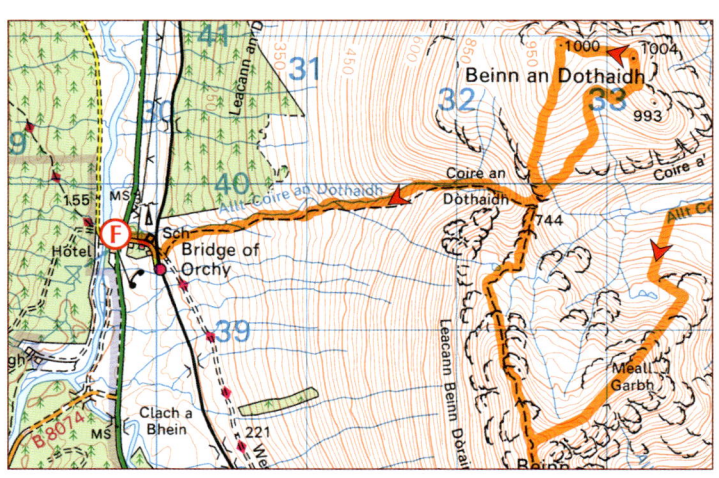

Route 8 – Hill Crossing: the back of Beinn Dorain

up to an intake dam on a stream. After crossing below this, the main track turns uphill, but contour forward on a rougher track to pass below a second intake dam, this gathering the waters of **Allt Coire a' Ghabhalach** (The Forking Corrie). Head upstream, on grassy slopes, into the corrie.

After a steepish start the stream line turns westwards and the slope is easier. At 610m, the valley levels, in what is probably a former lochan bed, with crags of Beinn an Dothaidh above on the right. Here turn up left, south, onto the northeast ridge of Beinn Dorain. Go up its rounded spur to **Meall Garbh**. A pleasant ridgeline with traces of a path runs to the north top of **Beinn Dorain**, with a big baggers' path leading south through a col to the summit.

Follow the path and ridgeline back north, and down to the col at the head of Coire an Dothaidh. The main path now turns down left towards Bridge of Orchy; but take a path slanting to the right (northeast) out of the col. It slants up a steepish slope, then fades onto the soggy slopes of a shallow south-facing hollow. Ahead is the 993m top above Beinn an Dothaidh's east ridge, and you can cross damp ground to reach this viewpoint. Then follow the ridgeline (airy on the right) to the 1004m main top of **Beinn an Dothaidh**. (It's only 1002m on the Harvey WH Way map).

Drop west around the top of the hollow, and then down a bit west of south, with the stream on your left, to find the path used on the ascent. Once back in the col between the two Munros turn down the steep eroded path west. At the floor of the corrie, the path descends to left of the stream, over peaty ground, to reach the WH Way track just above the railway and **Bridge of Orchy**.

Beinn Dorain's summit ridge

NOT THE WEST HIGHLAND WAY: A MOUNTAIN HIGH WAY

ROUTE 9
Inveroran Outing: Ben Inverveigh and Meall Tairbh

Start/finish	Inveroran
Distance	12km (7½ miles)
Ascent	650m (2200ft)
Approximate time	4.5hr
Maximum altitude	Meall Tairbh 665m
Terrain	Path for first ascent, then grassy hills

Throughout the 20th century the Inveroran Hotel was an occasional base for the Scottish Mountaineering Club. Members who arrived early would spend a few hours dashing up the two small hills that form such a natural circuit to the south, and descend to dinner with legs stretched ready for an icy adventure in the high corrie of Stob Ghabhar.

Small hills consist almost entirely of the rough stuff at the bottom, with hardly any top to compensate. Here, however, the WH Way and then

Beinn an Dothaidh and Beinn Dorain, from Meall Tairbh

ROUTE 9 – INVERORAN OUTING: BEN INVERVEIGH AND MEALL TAIRBH

a pretty good path get you up to the 500m mark. And the ridge of Ben Inverveigh compensates for lack of altitude by being both reasonably long, and friendly underfoot. Meall Tairbh offers another 2km of pleasant ground. Only the final descent is the typical low-hill roughness.

Meall Tairbh is in the unexciting category of Grahams: hills of 2000ft with 500ft of drop round. Inverveigh isn't even that as its drop is merely 144m. These are hills to be on for the pure pleasure of being on the hill. Use them in the afternoon after a morning walk from Tyndrum. Or make them a non-sedentary day at Inveroran before tomorrow's tough crossing of the Black Mount.

From just east of Inveroran Hotel, follow the WH Way up to its high point at **Mam Carraigh**. Just before the cairn to left of the path a wheelmark path turns off to the right (south). It runs up the ridgeline of Ben Inverveigh, shrinking to a path for the final rise to Point 546m. Here there are two TV repeater masts.

The small path continues southwest, but vanishes as the ridgeline broadens. That ridge is grassy with occasional pools, and leads gently up to **Ben Inverveigh**'s summit cairn. From here Meall Tairbh looks considerably lower. It is in fact 26m higher; the illusion is because of the much larger Ben Cruachan behind.

The ridge continues gently downhill, still grassy and still southwest. Follow it to its end, then turn down right to a wide, hummocky col. Pass to right of **Lochan**

NOT THE WEST HIGHLAND WAY: A MOUNTAIN HIGH WAY

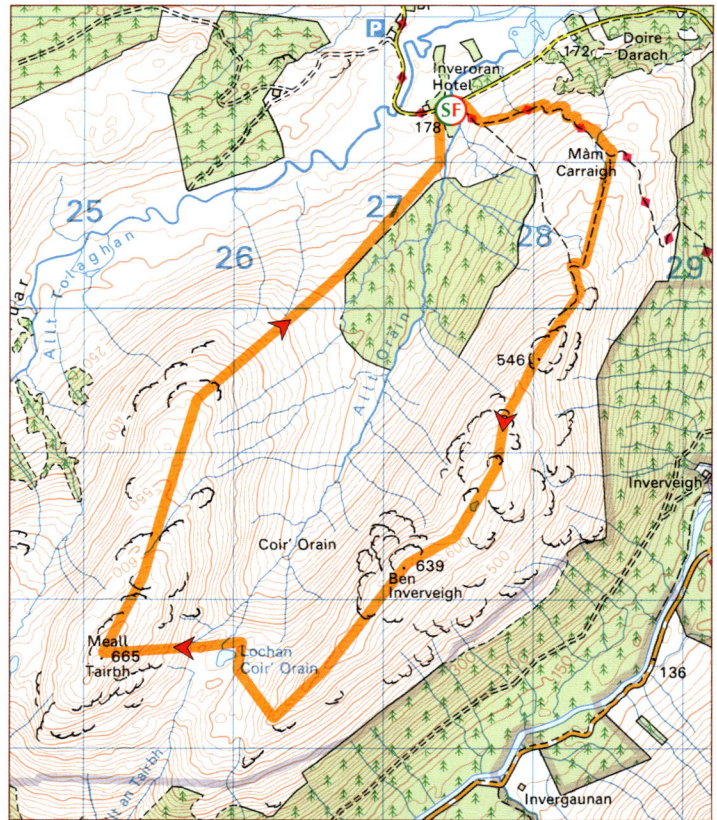

Coir' Orain to reach less peaty and heathery terrain, then make the steepish but short climb to **Meall Tairbh**. (Looking back now, it's Ben Inverveigh that looks to be far below you.)

The ridgeline runs down northeast. At the 500m contour it steepens, and the going is now rough. Slant down northeast towards **Allt Orain**, to join a deer fence. This has traces of path on its near side, but there are also soggy patches. When the fence turns away, keep ahead down the moorland directly to the **Inveroran Hotel**.

INVERORAN TO KINGS HOUSE

The end of yesterday gave a feeling of remoteness. Today is Rannoch, where the remoteness is real. This is the great bog of Scotland, where even the red deer gets stuck in a peat pool and suffocates to death. Rannoch Moor is a truly terrifying place.

Or at least it would be, if Mr Telford hadn't built a firm, stone-bedded roadway along the edge of it. That roadway gives a close-up view of the wavering grasses, the multicoloured acres of moss, the black peat and granite boulders and huge peaty pools.

And for the inspiring overview, head up onto the Black Mount. Three grand mountains emerge from a tangle of ridges and rocky corries. It's a magnificent crossing. The bonus is, unlike anybody else attempting it, you don't have to trek down the West Highland Way afterwards, in the dark, just to return to your car.

Inveroran Hotel and Stob Ghabhar

NOT THE WEST HIGHLAND WAY: A MOUNTAIN HIGH WAY

WH WAY: INVERORAN TO KINGS HOUSE

Distance	16km (10 miles)
Approximate time	4.5hr
Not the WH Way	Route 10: Hill Crossing: Black Mount

Below all this, the WH Way continues along the road past **Inveroran Hotel**, and over an unnamed bridge (informal camping here) and then Victoria Bridge, to Forest Lodge. To right of the lodge, pass through a gate onto Thomas Telford's stony-surfaced old road. This would be rather hard to get lost on. After 1km, pass above a plantation, and 2km later pass below another. After this one the road runs level, to pass to left of a third plantation, and then pass Lochan Mhic Pheadair Ruaidhe. Another 1km leads to stone-built **Ba Bridge**.

West Highland Way, north end of Rannoch Moor

INVERORAN TO KINGS HOUSE

In a few more steps the road is surfaced with rounded granite pebbles, and boulders of it are in the moor alongside. A side-track on the left leads up to the ruined Ba Cottage, and just after the following bridge a faint but followable path on the right would lead out to the A82. The old road climbs gently to a high point behind the moorland hump Beinn Chaorach (Sheep Hill). Above it, reached by 150 metres of peat path, is a memorial cairn to Peter Fleming, diplomat, adventurer, and brother of Ian Fleming the author. He was intending to shoot deer, and must have been surprised when he was the one that died.

The old road now drops gently towards Buachaille Etive Mor. A well-made side-path with an unnecessarily ugly signboard would lead to the café at the foot of the White Corries chairlift, but the main WH Way forks right and soon joins the chairlift access road at white-walled Blackrock Cottage. Turn right, to cross the A82. The roughly tarred old road continues across moorland to **Kings House Hotel**.

ROUTE 10
Hill Crossing: Black Mount

Start/finish	Inveroran
Finish	Kings House
Distance	22.5km (13 miles)
Ascent	1600m (5300ft)
Approximate time	9hr
Maximum altitude	Meall a' Bhuiridh 1108m
Terrain	Hill paths and pathless rough grass

Three large hills, linked by high ridges and rocky passes, all part of a huge and confusing highland massif. This is a big hillwalk – not just in time taken, but in seriousness and atmosphere. While it's not a fearsome challenge, it does make real demands on your stamina, navigation, scrambling (and as always your Gaelic pronunciation). Here is all the variety of the Highlands: a secluded stream valley, a hidden corrie complete with lochan, a high grassy plateau, bare granite slabs, steep slopes, and sharp ridgelines of stones and easy scrambling. So it's a quite unnecessary bonus that the Black Mount has a friendly pub at each end of it.

It is possible to include the lesser Munro, Stob a' Choire Odhair. This makes the crossing really pretty strenuous, and Stob Odhair is not the equal of the other three, so I prefer to leave it out. Return to it later in your mountain career, and it'll provide a perfect excuse for a revisit to great Stob Ghabhar.

An alternative end to the crossing is to descend directly north by the Sron na Creise – the 'nose' of Creise. This is the authentic ridgeline, and the descent weaves excitingly among steep crags before a harsh crossing of the moorland and a dodgy crossing of River Etive. Again, I leave this fine line as an excuse for a later revisit to cracking Creise.

Follow the road across Victoria Bridge to reach **Forest Lodge**. (The WH Way continues through a gate to right of this lodge.) In front of the lodge turn left along a track under pines, soon emerging into the open at a gate. Follow the track, with **River Shira** to your left, for about 1.5km, passing a plantation on your right. At

ROUTE 10 – HILL CROSSING: BLACK MOUNT

the start of a second plantation, and just after passing a tin hut, turn up right on a clear path.

This ascends to right of **Allt Toaig**. At the 400m level, the path crosses a sidestream, and just after this an eroded baggers' path sets off up Stob a' Choire Odhair, supposing you wanted to bag that one. The main path bends left and slants back towards Allt Toaig, as the valley itself bends left and unsteepens into its upper hollow. The path, now small, heads up to the col at the stream head.

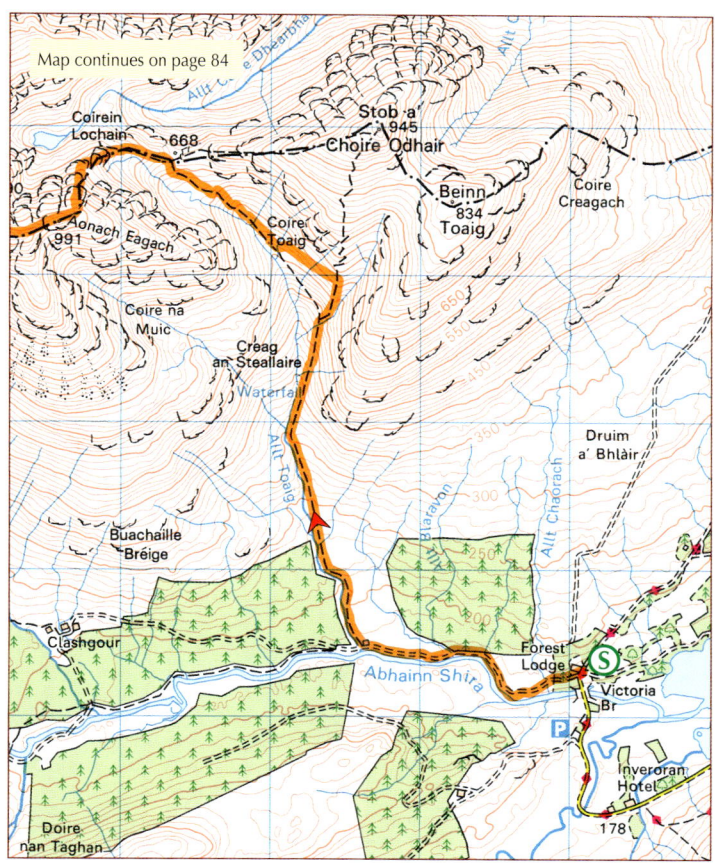

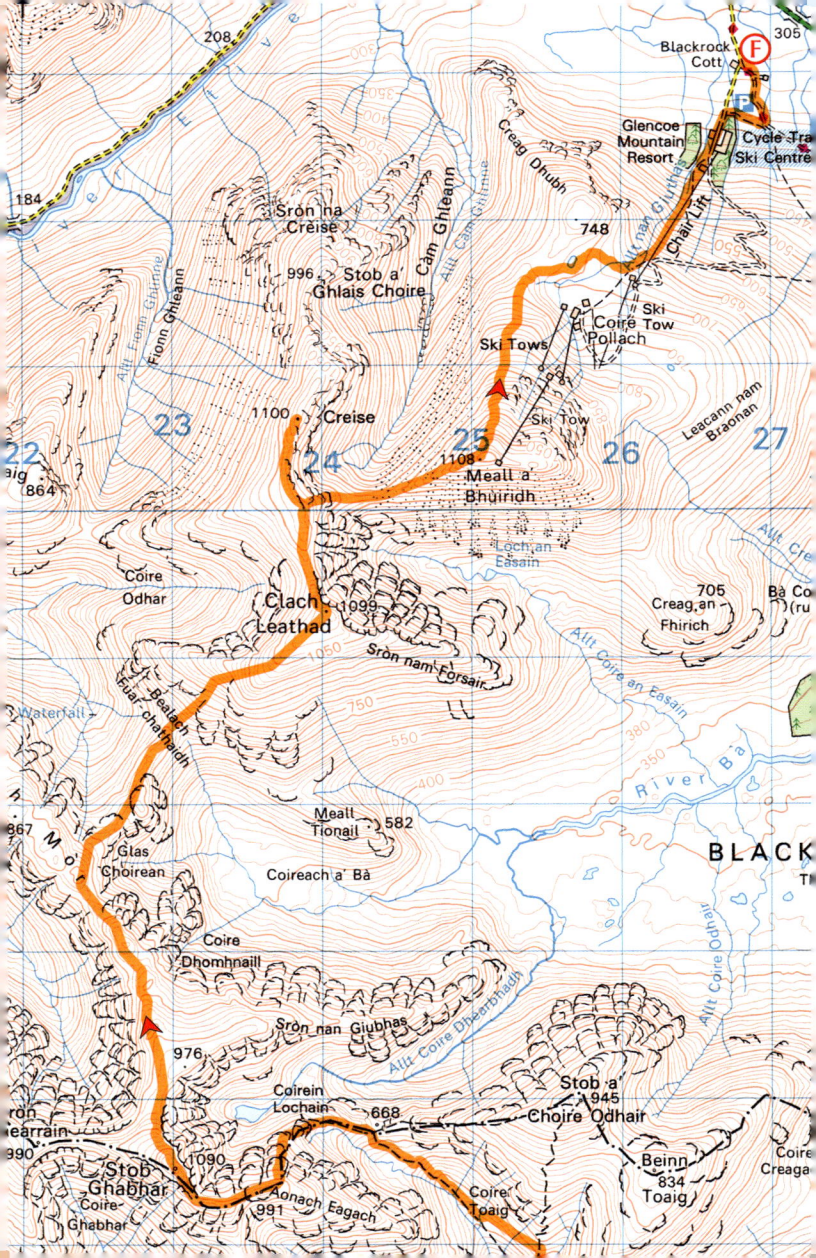

ROUTE 10 – HILL CROSSING: BLACK MOUNT

Here a path arrives from up right off Stob a' Choire Odhair. Follow it to the left, up a knobbly spur. There's some rock to scramble briefly, then bouldery bits, and places with a choice between bouldery and eroded-to-rock. The path arrives on the tip of the **Aonach Eagach** ridge. The famous Aonach Eagach (Notched Ridge) is above Glen Coe. This one is easier.

Head up the ridge, to where it narrows and becomes rocky. There's a path near the crest, with just a little scrambling. The ridge broadens to a rounded summit. Keep ahead, soon joined by the remains of a fence, which is followed up quite steeply to the summit of **Stob Ghabhar**. Stob Ghabhar, 'Stob Gower', is the Peak of the Goats.

The summit is blocky rhyolite, but as you head down northwest you return onto rounded whitish granite. A small path follows the rim of the northeast corrie to **Sron nan Giubhas**. (In mist, this very minor top at 976m pinpoints your change of direction. Otherwise you'll probably skirt it. From here to Bealach Fuar-chathaidh in mist requires care, or a GPS, or both.)

Now head gently down northwest over rough grassland. In thick weather, note the small lochan at the foot of the first descent (NN 2281 4773). Continue

Stob Ghabhar from head of Coire Toaig

through a slight further dip, then over a rise and down to a deeper col. Through this col the ridgeline becomes fairly narrow. From this col slant up right (north) to a rocky knoll with a cairn (NN 2238 4750).

Descend steeply northeast to a wide col floored in parts with bare granite, the **Bealach Fuar-chathaidh**. There are sheltered campsites with water just down to the left. Cross the hump Creag a' Bhealaich which interrupts the col. At the steep ground, slant up to the right for a minute or two to meet a stream. Follow it uphill to reach the west ridge of Clach Leathad.

Turn right, up the stony ridge, to **Clach Leathad** summit, with its large cairn. Clach Leathad means 'stony slope' (pronounced Clachlet). It used to be the Munro but now Creise is 2m higher. Like all the summits today, the rock at the top is rhyolite rather than granite.

Descend northwest at first to skirt crags, bending round north once down the steep summit knoll. Follow the stony ridge to the cairn on **Creise**.

Return south for 750 metres. There's a cairn on the ridge crest, and another on the left-hand (eastern) edge marking the top of the descent spur east (NN 2390

Aonach Eagach ridge of Stob Ghabhar

Route 10 – Hill Crossing: Black Mount

Ridgeline to Meall a' Bhuiridh

5001). The spur has a clear path, with some scrambling down short rock steps, to the long, narrow col leading towards Meall a' Bhuiridh. Follow this ridge to **Meall a' Bhuiridh** summit.

Descend north, on sketchy paths, down the edge of the ski area with ski warning signs to your left. At the 850m level head straight down to the foot of the ski lifts, with various buildings. Follow a track ahead past the Plateau Café to the top of the chairlift. The closure of the White Corries ski area is constantly prophesied, a victim of climate change. In theory (at least) the lifts and buildings would then be removed.

At the chairlift top, a sign 'Footpath' indicates the descent path, to left of the chairlift and then passing underneath it. As the slope steepens, the path becomes very eroded, to reach the bottom station of the chairlift, with its café and large car park.

Follow the access road out to the A82 and cross it onto the decomposing old road to Kings House.

Not the West Highland Way: A Mountain High Way

KINGS HOUSE TO KINLOCHLEVEN

Devil's Staircase, back to Buachaille Etive Mor

The Devil's Staircase is either the worst bit, or the best bit, of the West Highland Way. If you've bought this book, you'll be of the 'best bit' persuasion I guess. The path is wide and well made, originally by soldiers in 1750 under Major Caulfeild. It is, on the other hand, uphill. Its 250m of ascent is the longest on the Way, and comes just as the blister plasters are failing to contain the blisters of the first five days. But those who've spent days shorter in distance, on ground rougher and uphill, will find the mile of well-engineered zigzags rather relaxing.

The alternative route, over Beinn a' Chrulaiste, is only slightly higher. But it's altogether different because it lacks that engineered path. And if, since Loch Lomond, you've forgotten what it's like in a wood, it takes you through four miles of birch and oak trees above the River Leven.

WH WAY: KINGS HOUSE TO KINLOCHLEVEN

Distance	14km (9 miles)
Approximate time	4hr
Not the WH Way	Route 11: Hill Crossing: Beinn a' Chrulaiste and the Blackwater

Behind the Kings House Hotel the WH Way continues across a bridge over River Etive. Informal camping is along the riverside. After 300 metres turn left. Here the track for Beinn a' Chrulaiste (next route) and Rannoch Moor (Route 21) turns off right.

In another 1km the WH Way turns right off the minor road onto a roughish path. This slopes gently up the flank of Beinn a' Chrulaiste, then descends even more gently back to the A82. On this descent, you pass into the Glencoe Cauldron Subsidence, and see red rhyolite and dark grey andesite lavas in the path.

The path runs alongside the A82, its last encounter with this over-affectionate road. At **Altnafeadh** turn up right on the good footpath. Its final climb is the graded zigzags of the **Devil's Staircase**.

At the top are two cairns, and the sudden, stunning view of the Mamores hits you. Its swooping ridgeline is a wall across the northward view, with evening sun lingering on the triangular summits. The idea of climbing right over it (Routes 12 and 13) provides welcome distraction from the 4km of stony track down to Kinlochleven.

But even that stony downhill track is pretty good. With those great high hills alongside, it winds its way down a glen where, for the first time on the regular WH Way, no sign of human life intrudes. Here are no roads, buildings or power lines to entangle the eye; but bleak plateaux of peat, and grey rocks, and grass rising like a tidal wave to that high crest line, whitened by the evening sun and possibly also by a sprinkle of snow.

The good path descends gently, with level sections, then more steeply, to join a track above the top station of the hydroelectric downpipes. Turn down this smooth track, which zigzags through birch woods, passing below a small reservoir with a weir. Just above Kinlochleven it joins the pipeline, then crosses it.

The **Ice Factor** (former aluminium factory) is just ahead, along with the Blackwater Hostel, but the WH Way itself forks right on a rough track. This crosses some red rhyolite rock and then a bridge over River Leven – the rhyolite dyke is seen in the riverbed immediately upstream. Keep ahead in Wade Road (credit where it's due, this should be Caulfeild Road) for 400 metres, then turn left on a tarred path that runs alongside the river. It passes the tailrace, exit water from the hydroelectric power plant, then reaches the road bridge in the middle of **Kinlochleven**.

NOT THE WEST HIGHLAND WAY: A MOUNTAIN HIGH WAY

ROUTE 11
Hill Crossing: Beinn a' Chrulaiste and the Blackwater

Start	Kings House
Finish	Kinlochleven
Distance	16km (10 miles)
Ascent	650m (2200ft)
Approximate time	5.5hr
Maximum altitude	Beinn a' Chrulaiste 857m
Terrain	Pathless hill, a rough boggy bit to Blackwater dam, and then a woodland path

Beinn a' Chrulaiste – it's not very high, it's almost entirely crag-free, and you have to ask what such a grassy hump is doing right in the middle of the Glencoe mountains and under the shadow of the Mamores. Well, it's supplying a grand viewpoint, that's one thing. To feet and legs that have had enough, for now, of great steep slopes, it also offers a grassy stream valley, an ascent of merely 600m, and an afternoon wander through a wood and some waterfalls. And for those who insist on vertigo-inducing drops alongside the path, there's the concrete crossing of the Blackwater dam.

The Mamores from the Devil's Staircase path

ROUTE 11 – HILL CROSSING: BEINN A' CHRULAISTE AND THE BLACKWATER

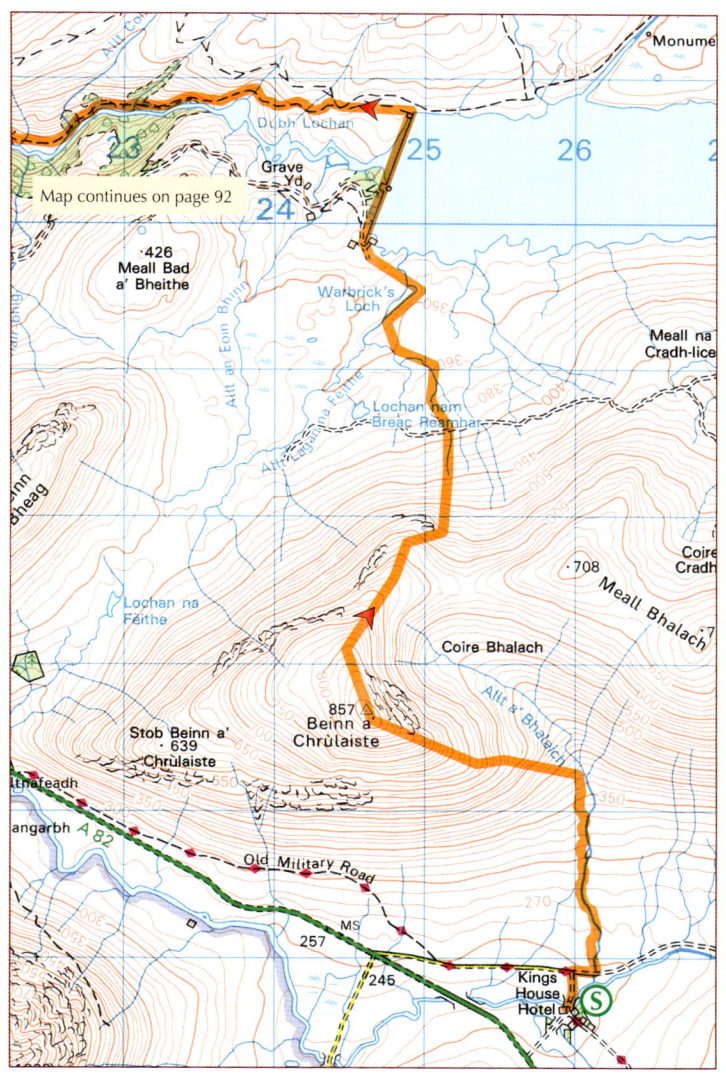

NOT THE WEST HIGHLAND WAY: A MOUNTAIN HIGH WAY

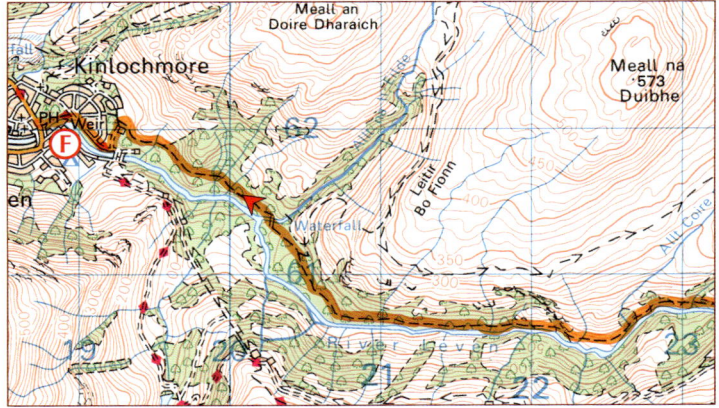

Follow the old road to its corner just north of **Kings House**.

Turn right through a gate onto the track towards Black Corries Lodge. Ignore one faint, boggy path striking up to the left. Instead follow the track for 200 metres to cross the stream **Allt a' Bhalaich**. Go up a small but useful path alongside the stream (on its left initially). Pass under power lines, and pass a ruined shieling at 340m.

Don't be in any hurry to leave the stream, which runs prettily over pink rhyolite and pale grey granite alternately. As the stream steepens, the path is on its left. Another 500 metres beyond the shieling, at altitude 410m, the stream bends right in a small gorge; here leave it and strike up the east spur of Beinn a' Chrulaiste. This is pathless but not rough.

Buachaille Etive Mor and Beag from Warbrick's Loch above Blackwater Reservoir

ROUTE 11 – HILL CROSSING: BEINN A' CHRULAISTE AND THE BLACKWATER

Beinn a' Chrulaiste summit has a concrete pillar trig. Head down the plateau slightly west of north. The broad spurline bends gradually right, to northeast. Don't swing east down to a wide col but follow the spurline down northeast until it steepens at 580m. Slant down to right of the spur's steep end, still northeast, into Coire Garbh.

Follow grassy stream banks down out of the corrie, then head north across rough moorland, following the largest stream for the slightly better drained ground on its banks. The stream eventually leads to **Warbrick's Loch**, a former reservoir with a broken concrete dam. Cross the stream below, and head left above the reservoir to the end of the **Blackwater dam**. The track ahead, along the left side of the valley, is an easy but uninteresting way to Kinlochleven.

Crossing the dam requires climbing over an entrance gate marked 'no admittance'. On my reading of it, the Scottish Access Code explicitly permits dam crossings; but if deterred either by the notice or by the big drop, a crossing can be made on rough ground below the dam.

At the dam's end, turn left to follow a path below a water pipeline. After 400 metres, the path forks. Keep down left for the Chiaran path, which runs above two small lochans and then through woods above **River Leven**. The pipeline and its accompanying path could also be followed, for 5km, to a steep spur path down westwards. It has grand views but I prefer the woodland path below.

After 4km look out for a short peaty spur path on the right to view the waterfall of Allt na h-Eilde. Then the main path drops to the footbridge over that stream. In 1km, above the edge of Kinlochleven, fork down left, on the main path. After a gateway in deer fencing it drops to a track. The WH Way's bridge over River Leven is just to the left. Cross that for the Blackwater Hostel; or else follow the WH Way ahead to the main road bridge in **Kinlochleven**.

NOT THE WEST HIGHLAND WAY: A MOUNTAIN HIGH WAY

KINLOCHLEVEN TO FORT WILLIAM

From Loch Lomond all the way to Rannoch Moor the West Highland Way followed a single great valley. The river in the bottom was the Fillan, or the Finnan, or the Orchy; but 20,000 years ago it was one big glacier out of Rannoch.

Above Kings House there was a ridge to cross, through the gap of the Devil's Staircase or over the low hill alongside. Now, a larger and more impressive ridgeline blocks the way. The Mamores are major mountains. Even the easiest way across will take you to the 1000m contour, right up among the summits.

There is, however, a valley slot passing westwards, right around the end. That the Lairig Mor is there is just as well for the West Highland Way, which otherwise couldn't exist. But in every other way, it's a shame. So pretend that the great ridgeline of the Mamores is a necessary obstacle, and make that high mountain passage through to Glen Nevis.

On the other hand, the Mamores also have a right-hand end. Route 15 heads up past Loch Eilde, around by Abhainn Rath, and down along Glen Nevis. It's remote and roundabout, but not especially high or rugged; and upper Glen Nevis is lovely with its big waterfall and gorge.

WH WAY: KINLOCHLEVEN TO FORT WILLIAM

Distance	23km (14 miles)
Approximate time	6.5hr
Not the WH Way	Route 12: Hill Crossing: Mamores
	Route 12a: Hill Crossing: More Mamores (Am Bodach)
	Route 14: Fort William Outing: Ben Nevis by the CMD Arête

But it's raining, and your feet are sore, and you want the least energetic way, which is the West Highland one. Then leave **Kinlochleven** on the road towards Onich and Fort William. After a school, a path with a metal signpost forks right, up into woodland. This path climbs fairly relentlessly. At the tarred access road for Mamore Lodge cross to the continuing path opposite. Slabs of off-white, sharp-cornered quartzite are above the path as it zigzags to join a track above.

Turn left on this, as it contours high above Loch Leven, then heads gently uphill into the pass behind Beinn na Caillich. This, the Lairig Mor or 'Big Pass', is a green and beige place, silent below big hills. For the first time in the walk, you're a

Kinlochleven to Fort William

few hours' walk from the A82 or any other road. There are no pipes or pylons. The signs of man are the ruins of ancient summer pastures, and a broken house called **Tigh na Sleubhaich**, and the track running through.

As the track descends past the ruin, the valley ahead appears to have no exit, but the large stream runs downhill ahead and must get out somehow. In fact the valley bends round to the right. The track gradually drops to a signboard at Campbell's Cairn (see page 179 for the bloody history), and enters forestry plantations recently clear-felled.

Opposite **Lochan Lunn Da Bhra**, a small shelter and noticeboard indicate a short-cut to Fort William by the public road ahead. But fork up right on the well-made path, climbing through more clear-felled plantation, then across open moor. Ben Nevis looms ahead, until the path enters plantations. It contours, dips sharply to cross a stream, climbs again, and emerges to a wide, smooth, forest road.

After a couple of hundred metres, as the view opens ahead, the forest road dips and there are paths off both ways. That on the right is the diversion to **Dun Deardail**.

Small hill side-trip: Dun Deardail

Dun Deardail is a fine viewpoint, but further away than the optimistic sign says and a stiff little climb. The path soon emerges from the trees, then slants up onto the hill fort. There are traces of vitrified stonework around the rim. To the east you look steeply into the depths of the glen, and across to the great high side of Ben Nevis. Linger in its grassy hollow, sheltered by what's left of the vitrified stonework, then return to the WH Way by the same path.

Kinlochleven

NOT THE WEST HIGHLAND WAY: A MOUNTAIN HIGH WAY

Directly opposite the Dun Deardail turn-off is an old path that slightly short-cuts the first wide bend downhill of the forest road. After rejoining that road briefly, the old path drops off to the right, letting you short-cut the second of the wide descending bends.

The wide, smooth road descends past a roadstone quarry and bends back to the left, to contour above **Glen Nevis** through felled plantation. After 1.5km it joins a lower track. Here you could turn back sharp right for 400 metres for a track descending to the youth hostel. But the main WH Way continues ahead, down-valley, for another 600 metres. Ahead now is a direct route to Fort William by the Braveheart car park and a woodland path.

Now the WH Way's waymarked path turns right, downhill. Emerging from the plantation it passes an old graveyard (worth a brief visit through a gate on the left). The path ahead crosses between fields to the Glen Nevis road.

Turn left. After 200 metres a path forking off right leads to the **Nevis Centre**. Here the WH Way is determined on tarmac for its final 2km and forges on along the road. You can make a much pleasanter end to the path by turning aside to pass the Nevis Centre for a footbridge at the corner of its car park. Cross to the right bank of **River Nevis**, for a riverside path downstream. After 1.5km recross by a green metal bridge, and rejoin the WH Way to the nondescript roundabout that until 2010 marked its final point. Today's waymarks continue ahead, to turn left along Fort William's pedestrianised main street. There's a 'wee man wi' sair feet' to photograph yourself beside, before carrying your till-starved credit card into the surrounding shops.

Ben Nevis from Dun Deardail

ROUTE 12

Hill Crossing: Mamores

Start	Grey Mare's car park, Kinlochleven
Finish	Fort William
Distance	20.5km (13 miles)
Ascent	1000m (3300ft)
Approximate time	7.5hr
Maximum altitude	Sgorr an Iubhair 1001m
Terrain	Hill paths, with a mostly gentle descent; then a small inconspicuous path along River Nevis

The high crossing of the Mamores is a short-cut – of sorts. There are paths, well graded and built by deer stalkers, even if nowadays rather eroded. Purists will enjoy the way that the easiest line actually passes sideways over one of the summits – and that summit, at over 1000m, is even so not one of the necessary ones listed in *Munro's Tables*: Sgurr an Iubhair was deleted in 1997.

The impure, who like to knock off those necessary Munro summits, can consider a more extended ridge walk that takes in two of them.

It's a shame to leave Kinlochleven by a way which doesn't pass the waterfall. So while the WH Way would be a short-cut, take instead the broad path behind the Grey Mare's car park, turning left to follow the coloured waymarks. After a footbridge, divert to the left for 100 metres to visit the foot of the waterfall. Then return past the footbridge for the steep uphill path.

At the top of the birch wood is a path junction. The longer 'More Mamores' route (see below) and Route 13 (Between the Binneins) turn off here. Here turn left, with a white waymark. Cross a footbridge and head up past a white house. The path emerges near **Mamore Lodge** hotel.

Above the hotel take the track to the left, high above Loch Leven. After 2km the **WH Way** joins from below. In another 500 metres a path sets off uphill to the right; the start of the path is just behind some rock slabs, and not all that obvious.

The path runs up to left of a stream. After 1km it crosses it, but stays beside it, before zigzagging up to the gap between Sgurr an Iubhair (left) and Am Bodach (right). 'More Mamores' rejoins this route at the col.

At the col, do not descend ahead (north). To do so would take you down into Coire a' Mhail, a hanging valley that leads out onto the precipices alongside

NOT THE WEST HIGHLAND WAY: A MOUNTAIN HIGH WAY

Steall Waterfall. Instead turn left (northwest) along the ridgeline path, which rises gradually to the stony summit of **Sgurr an Iubhair**. This was deleted from Munro's Tables because it was considered not to be separate enough from slightly higher mountains nearby.

Descend northwest, on a steep and sketchy path that soon leads to a wide saddle. Ahead is the Devil's Ridge of Sgurr a' Mhaim: tough, but fun. The descent northwest from Sgurr a' Mhaim is long and rather steep. If your knees can cope, it's a great way to Glen Nevis.

For an altogether easier route than the Devil's Ridge ahead, turn down left on a zigzag path to a small, sheltered lochan – Lochan Coire nam Miseach on some

Below Am Bodach

maps. The path crosses the lochan outflow and contours forward (west), after 400 metres meeting the ridge crest just above. At this point turn down to the right on a well-used path. This is fairly gentle, with a couple of steeper eroded sections to contend with. It runs right down Coire a' Mhusgain, with the wooded stream below, great mountainsides rising on either side.

The car park in **Glen Nevis** is a bus stop for Fort William. But you can also walk it, away from the road, on the river's right bank. Cross the bridge on your right, and take the track on the left to pass **Polldubh** cottage onto a faint path. This

Crossing the Mamores ridgeline east of Stob Ban

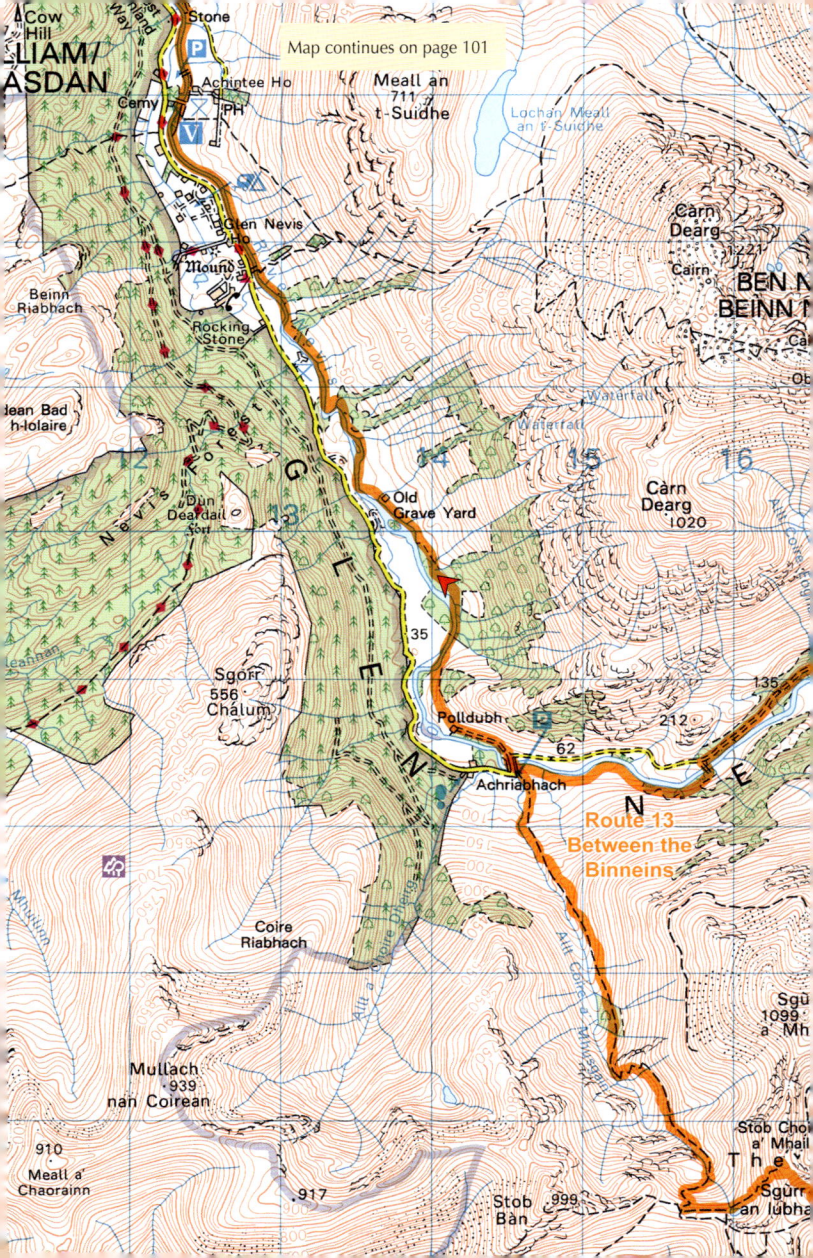

ROUTE 12 – HILL CROSSING: MAMORES

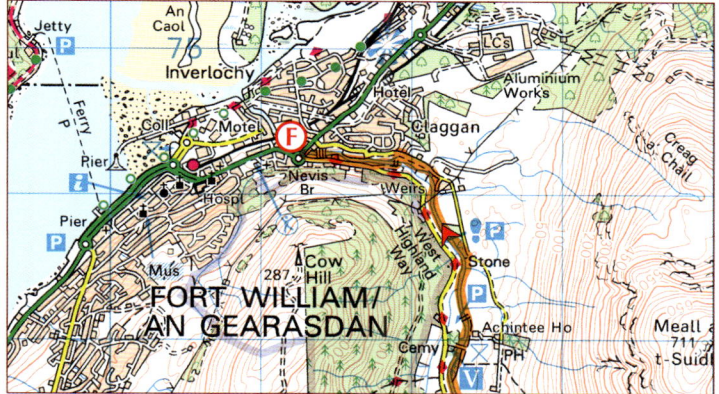

soon joins River Nevis, and follows it all the way down the glen. After 3.5km you cross two substantial burns running down off Ben Nevis. Soon afterwards you pass a first footbridge across River Nevis (if crossed, it would take you to the youth hostel) and 1.5km after that another would lead over to the Nevis Centre. But stay on the right bank for its pleasant path. In 400 metres bear left on a path which passes Roaring Mill pool to the edge of **Claggan.**

Cross a green metal footbridge over River Nevis, and turn right to join the Glen Nevis road. Just ahead is the roundabout at the edge of **Fort William**, with a sign which used to mark the official end of the West Highland Way. Since 2010 you must walk an extra mile into the town's main shopping centre.

More Mamores – Route 12a

Given good weather and good legs, you could take in a stretch of the wonderful high ridgeline. Above Grey Mare's waterfall, turn off on the path uphill, roughly north, to join a high track. Follow this briefly to the left for the old stalkers' path up into the valley hollow of Allt Coire na Ba. Once on the high ridgeline at the 783m col, rough paths lead over Stob Coire a' Chairn and Am Bodach to the following col, where you meet the main route.

Following this onwards to Fort William gives a day of 20.5km (13 miles) with 1000m of ascent, about 7.5hr. Alternatively you can make this a circuit out of Kinlochleven; turn left down the main route (the very top of the path is unclear) back to the town. (15km/9.5miles with 1200m ascent, about 6hr).

Pap of Glencoe and Loch Leven seen from above Kinlochleven

Not the West Highland Way: A Mountain High Way

ROUTE 13
Hill Crossing: Between the Binneins

Start	Grey Mare's car park, Kinlochleven
Finish	Fort William *(or Glen Nevis YH)*
Distance	27.5km (17 miles) *(24km (15 miles) to Glen Nevis YH)*
Ascent	850m (2800ft)
Approximate time	8.5hr
Maximum altitude	Lochan between the Binneins 750m
Terrain	Hill paths, mostly good; rough pathless descent into Glen Nevis; potentially tricky river crossing; rougher paths to finish

There's a more devious way through the Mamores: a surprising and very beautiful route that uses old deer-stalkers' paths to thread among the summits at the range's eastern end and then a pathless descent into the wild and exciting upper part of Glen Nevis.

That descent is the tricky bit. The river at the bottom is crossable in normal summer conditions: but after heavy rain, or in winter, there may be no safe crossing, leaving you a diversion upstream. Once across it, there's still the long (and yes, very lovely) descent of the whole of Glen Nevis. Look exhausted enough, and you might just pick up a lift onwards from the upper car park…

Sgor Eilde Beag, and Sgor Eilde Mor; the route heads through the gap between them

Route 13 – Hill Crossing: Between the Binneins

Leaving Kinlochleven towards the Mamores

Start as Route 12 to the top edge of the birchwoods. Keep right here, up to a gate in deer fencing. The path contours north above **Allt Coire na Ba**, across two streams to another junction. Here turn right again, to pass out through the deer fence again and reach a broad smooth track with fabulous views.

Turn right along the track for 1km (3/4 mile), to a clear, stony path forking up to the left. Your last chance here to transfer into the longer, but much more

Map continues on page 109

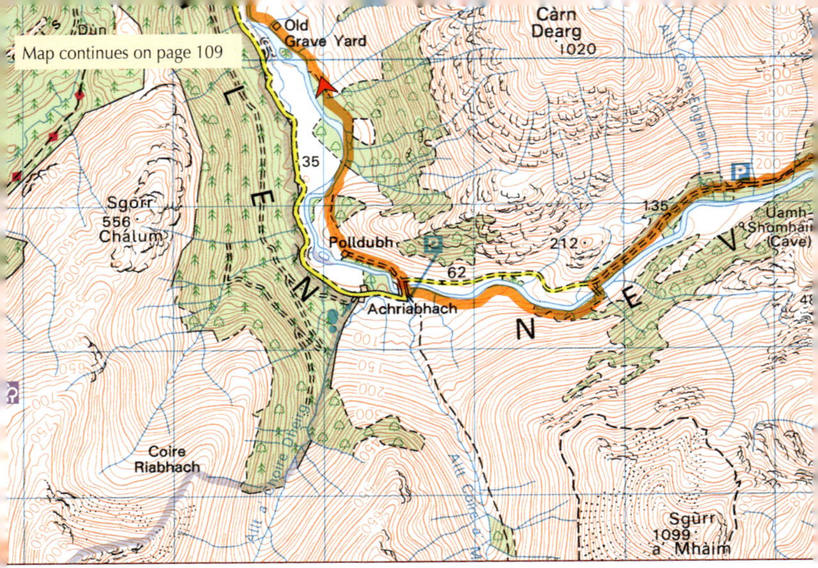

straightforward, Route 15 ('The back of Ben Nevis'). It slants around the southern spur of **Sgor Eilde Beag**. Watch out for where the most-used path turns directly uphill; here you want the fainter one that contours forward, below the very steep eastern flank, to **Coire an Lochain**, the wide saddle between the two Sgurr Eildes.

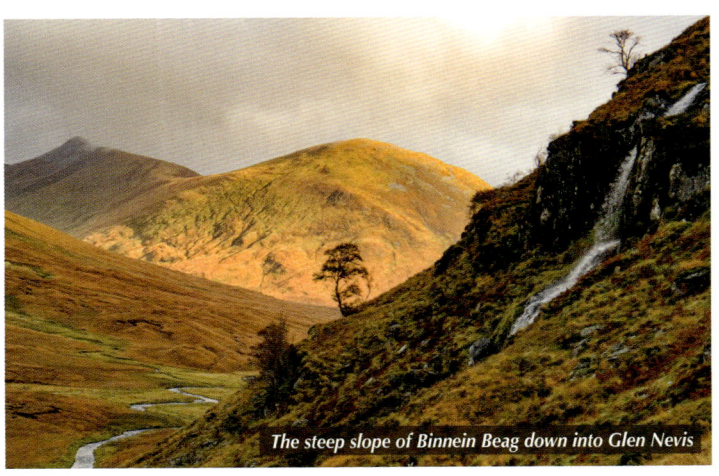

The steep slope of Binnein Beag down into Glen Nevis

NOT THE WEST HIGHLAND WAY: A MOUNTAIN HIGH WAY

The path passes to left of the main lochan then down northwest to cross a stream. It contours around the head of the hidden back valley **Coire a' Bhinnein**, then climbs to the wide saddle between Binnein Mor and Binnein Beag.

After passing to left of the unnamed lochan here, the path becomes very faint. If you have GPS, it's worth using it here to stay on the old pathline. Head north onto the west flank of **Binnein Beag**, and work down its northern slopes. The old path ends at a tiny knoll at the 550m contour. From here slant down northwest, to cross the **Water of Nevis** at the top of its wide S-bend (NN 213 688).

A rough path leads down-valley to the meadow below the **Steall Waterfall**. From here a well-made path leads above Nevis Gorge to the upper car park. Head down the road for 1.5km to cross a footbridge down left and a path downstream to the lower falls. Turn right across the river, for the rough but pretty path down-valley past **Polldubh** and all the way to the Youth Hostel footbridge or the edge of Fort William.

Sgurr a' Mhaim rises above Glen Nevis

Route 13 – Hill Crossing: Between the Binneins

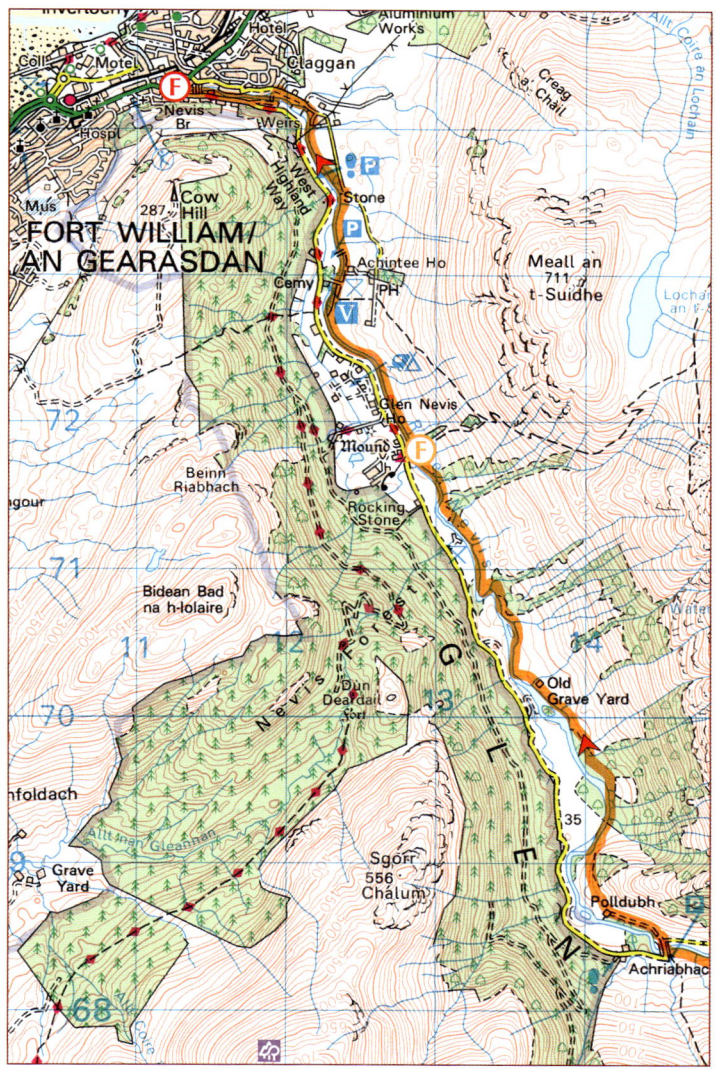

ROUTE 14
Fort William Outing: Ben Nevis by the CMD Arête

Start/finish	Nevis Bridge, Fort William
Distance	23km (14½ miles)
Ascent	1500m (5000ft)
Approximate time	9hr
Maximum altitude	Ben Nevis 1343m
Terrain	Hill paths, narrow rocky ridge, steep boulderfield, and a good path to descend

The West Highland Way is a demanding, but popular, walk. The walk up Ben Nevis by the Pony Path (or 'Mountain Trail') is tough too. And it carries around 100,000 ascenders a year – five times as many as the busy WH Way.

That route, although arduous, is a well-built path for much of the way up, then across a stony plateau. The view is of the caravan parks of Glen Nevis. One is almost unaware of the tremendous crags, the largest hunk of bare rock in Britain, lurking over the left-hand edge of the plateau.

But if, as I hope, you have found this book's high and wild ways above the West Highland Way even better than the real thing, you'll also want the wild way up Ben Nevis. The Carn Mor Dearg Arête is a succession of granite boulders strung across the sky. It's more of a clamber than an actual scramble; there are no technical difficulties (unless its snowy, or windy). But it is a serious place. You're almost 1000m up (over 3000ft), and there's no way down until you get to the end and slog up the long boulderslope to the summit of Ben Nevis itself. All the way along, supposing it's clear, you are gazing at that magnificent northern rockface. And if it's cloudy, that cloud swirls among the boulders in a way that's almost as impressive as what you'd see if you could see the scenery ahead and below.

Head out of **Fort William** on the A82 (Inverness) for 2km to the Ben Nevis distillery. Pass between the buildings, heading round to the left, to find a path alongside the **Allt a' Mhuillin** (stream). It passes under the railway, then through scrubby trees, to meet a track. Turn left on this for 200 metres, then fork right up the main track. It zigzags to a junction at 250m altitude.

ROUTE 14 – FORT WILLIAM OUTING: BEN NEVIS BY THE CMD ARÊTE

On the Carn Mor Dearg Arête; the snow cover is not unusual for May

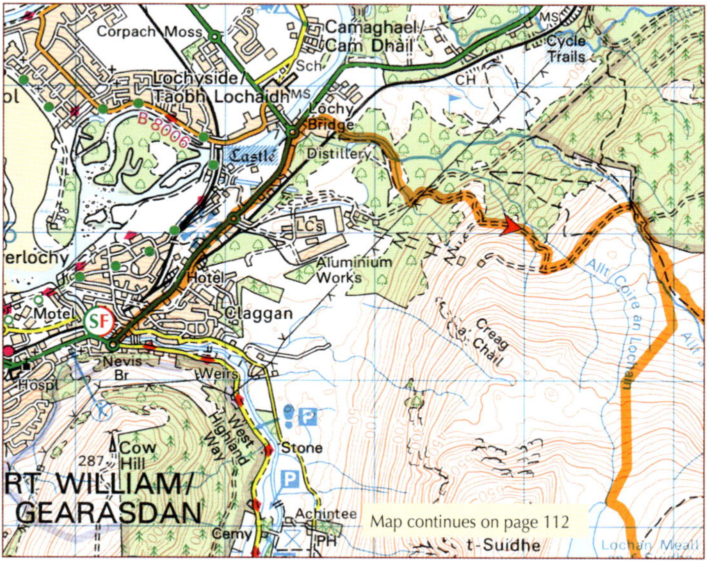

NOT THE WEST HIGHLAND WAY: A MOUNTAIN HIGH WAY

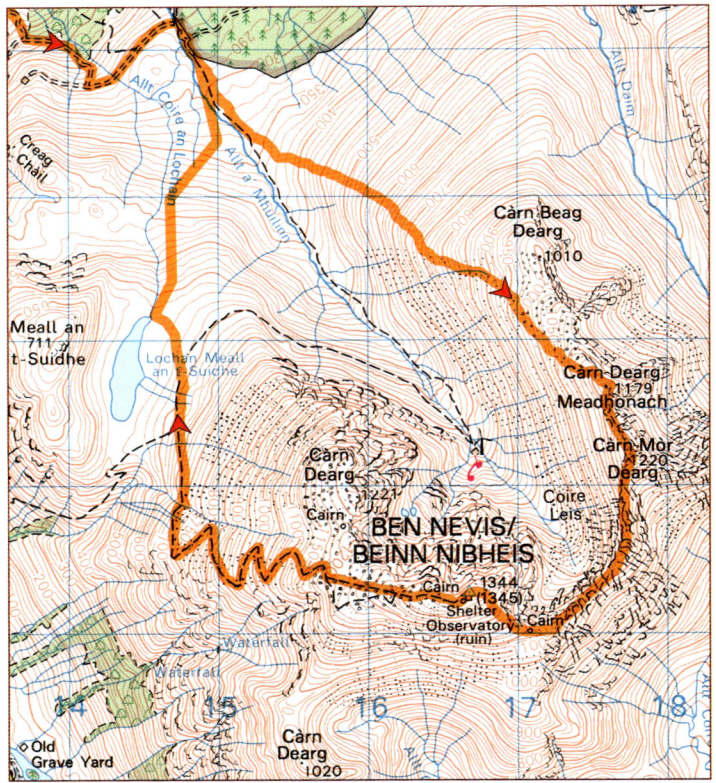

Turn left, around the hillside, for 400 metres, to cross a stream into trees. A wide ladder stile up on the right leads to a rebuilt path uphill. This heads into the great northern corrie of Ben Nevis.

As the path enters the hollow, bear off up the grassy slopes on the left. Follow them all the way up to the top called **Carn Beag Dearg**. The ridge runs forward over **Carn Dearg Meadhonach** to **Carn Mor Dearg**. Carn Mor Dearg: 'stonepile large and reddish-brown' (pronounced Carn Mor Jerrack). The reddish-brown comes from the outer Ben Nevis granite; five reddish 'Carn Dearg's are scattered around the big grey-black hill.

ROUTE 14 – FORT WILLIAM OUTING: BEN NEVIS BY THE CMD ARÊTE

A well-trodden spur now runs down southwards. Soon it narrows to the **Carn Mor Dearg Arête**, a ridgeline of jammed boulders. The rock is rough and gives good grip even when wet. But in strong winds this is an alarming place to be, and snow or ice makes it into a genuine winter climb. For those in balmy summer who're enjoying the clambering, there's plenty of it, as the ridge swings across the head of the northern corrie and eventually runs into the bouldery steep side of Ben Nevis.

Head straight up the bouldery slope, on various small zigzag paths, until you arrive at the ugly structures marking the summit of **Ben Nevis**.

Usually the Mountain Trail down the mountain's northwest flank is marked by a stream of people coming up it. There is also a line of cairns. In thick cloud, you may need compass bearings. From the trig point, head southwest for 150 metres. At this point you're around the head of Observatory Gully, and can turn half-right, on a bearing of 283°, along a line of newly-built cairns. Through the 2020s this is both the true bearing and also the magnetic one. Subtract 1° for every 6 years after 2024.

Ben Nevis from Corpach. The Mountain Trail takes the right-hand flank, unaware of the great precipices on the north (left in this picture) side

Not the West Highland Way: A Mountain High Way

This bearing will take you along the plateau and down the flank, where you'll pick up the wide zigzags of the Mountain Path. In summer conditions the various crags one might drop over on the right are visible whenever you get close enough. Slightly more care needs to be taken on the left, where the ground steepens gradually but inexorably into the trap of Five Finger Gully. Sometimes in winter, with snow cornices hanging out over the crags, the path covered over, and white cloud indistinguishable from white ground below, this descent becomes a serious – even a life-or-death – struggle.

The wide path zigzags down, its final swing to the right taking it across the Red Burn just below a small waterfall. The path continues slanting to the right, down towards the Halfway Plateau with its loch. Just above the plateau, the main path turns back sharp left, with a smaller (but still well-built) path ahead. That smaller path is the one you want to take, keeping ahead across the Halfway Plateau. Soon the well-built path forks off left. Follow this down to the northern end of the halfway loch (**Lochan Meall an t-Suidhe**). Keep on down the wide grassy slope, north. Eventually you cross the **Allt a' Mhuillin** stream, and rejoin the upward path just above the ladder stile at the top of the forest.

PART TWO
Beginnerish Backpacking

Vaude Scorpion tent in Coire an Lochain of Ben Lui (Route 19)

Supper at Sandwood Bay

You like hills. So why always make them a one-day event? If you really, really like them, surely you want to spend the night together?

You like camping – except when you look out in the morning and see all the other campers and their cars. So why not camp where it's really wild and exciting?

There are some obvious answers to those two questions. Such as: having a car to go home in means you can dry your socks; and a campsite has showers, and a shop selling ice cream, and even a toilet or two. Here we'll ignore the fact that wild camping means carrying a rather large rucksack simply in order to end up inside an excessively tiny tent. We'll assume that you've seen all the lovely pictures later in this book and decided it might be fun anyway. (And you're right, it is.)

Where should you start? I suggest that you get yourself and your rather large rucksack up to a big patch of country that's roughly south and east of Fort William. It's not a tame and small-scenery area: on the contrary, it contains Ben Cruachan, Ben Nevis, and the mighty mountains of Glen Coe. When you're in the middle of it, you are genuinely a long way from anywhere else. But at the same time it offers a lot to make you feel at home (in so far as a patch of peaty heather and a sheltering boulder can be considered home). The hills may be big, but the glens between have pretty good paths, really lovely rivers, and grassy-green camping spots. The middle of it all may be wild and empty, but the edge is only one more day's walk away. And if that edge is Kinlochleven, then there's a warm bunkhouse with a drying room, a late-opening shop, a couple of pubs, and a bus out to Ballachulish roadside and Glasgow.

You won't want that bus out to Glasgow. Northwards runs a rugged little path, and a tree-lined glen with waterfalls and tiny crags – they told you Scotland's bleak, but they lied. Well, Loch Treig is bleak, and so is upper Glen Nevis. But lower Glen Nevis is one of the grandest places anywhere. And if three days under the rucksack has stiffened your back, just the exercise you need is stretching high overhead to see the top of the Steall Waterfall.

There are also purely practical reasons to like Lochaber. If you should accidentally tear your tent apart while opening a tin of beans; if the loch should rise in the night and come in over your groundsheet; there is alternative shelter. The northern part of the area, in particular, is dotted with bothies. These simple, unlocked shelters ('for all who love the wild and empty places') have various disadvantages. Their wooden platforms make hard beds, inconsiderate other users may have left them slightly squalid, inconsiderate other users may be still there and laughing loudly all night at each other's fart jokes. They also have various advantages; the waterproof roof, in particular, but also the interesting company, who if they've hauled in fuel for the fire you might even forgive them the fart jokes. When you unfold the tent to find you left behind the tent pole, there's nothing more comforting than somewhere with a roof on just down the valley.

Finally, Lochaber has infrastructure. If you don't know whether you're the sort to carry 11 days' food along the John Muir Trail, Lochaber's where you aren't going to find out. Two days on the trail will bring you to a shop and yes, that shop sells tent poles. At start and end there's a railway, or else the convenient Citylink coach to Glasgow. There's even a railway in the middle: Corrour Station lies right off the road system at the corner of Rannoch Moor.

So if you're thinking of backpacking, Lochaber really could be the place to start. The overview maps at the beginning of the book show just how many routes there are to choose from; they'll be explored in Part Three. Later in this section are two two-day options, both of them easy to get to, easy to get home from, and not all that difficult in between.

THE EXCITEMENT IS IN TENTS

As you'll see from the pictures in this book, I'm a skinny weakling who likes to carry as little as possible. There are various small luxuries, weighing only a few grammes, that can make that tent evening at the riverside really special. But the big luxury is simply sitting around without the rucksack on. Simple sitting is such fun that rummaging in the sack for the bluetooth earbuds to tap into the Mozart chamber music may actually be less fun than that. If we want stimulation, there's the river to gaze into… And the other big luxury is laying the head down on whatever spare clothes are serving as a pillow and falling, deliciously, asleep.

You on the other hand may have legs like chunks of knotty bog oak; and the more you carry, the bigger and more bog-oak-like those legs are going to grow. In that case you'll want to carry everything you can. And when at evening your rucksack crashes to the ground like a mighty boulder, the very first thing you do – before unfolding the intricacies of your spacious double-skin tent – is to lower the six-pack of beer into the lochan to get cool.

Anything I might say about that spacious double-skin tent will be pure hearsay, perhaps tinged with envy. I can no more tell you what tent than I can tell you what house to inhabit when you get home again. Whatever you end up in, on a first backpack trip, you'll get several aspects of it wrong. It'll be too heavy, and too tricky to pitch. It'll certainly be too large (when it's inside the rucksack); it'll also be too small (when you're inside it). It's not airy enough, so the condensation can't get out; it's too airy, and the midges can get in.

PART 2 – BEGINNERISH BACKPACKING

Romantic camping in the northwest Highlands: Coire na Poite of Beinn Bhan, Applecross (Route 24)

The sordid stable at Loch Dochard carried a story pencilled on its wall of two campers who got almost everything right. They had carried their tent in without undue suffering, put it up with all the pegs in the appropriate places, crawled inside it and gone to sleep. Their mistake was in their preferred pitch. In the night came rain – a lot of rain. The lake came crawling up, and joined them inside the tent.

But the final, fundamental thing they did get right was being beside the sordid stable. Instead of spending the rest of the night trying to repitch the tent in the dark, in a strong wind, with everything wet – they were able to spend it inside the sordid stable, pencilling their sad story onto the wall.

In backpacking – as in life – the heavy loads fall upon those least able to bear them. I mean the brave young people of the Duke of Edinburgh scheme. They were told – by some unreliable eccentrics with tweedy breeches who can't even operate a remote control, let alone the latest smartphone technology, that a long walk would be just the thing. They bravely set out into the wet countryside, carrying gaiters and billy-cans, huge but chilly sleeping bags, beans in tins, and cheap, porous, superweight tents wrapped in black bin-liners. On a lightweight running

Heading up Glen Nevis from Steall (Route 15)

trip across the Southern Uplands we caught up with a group of these disadvantaged youngsters. Any social interaction would have been us looking pityingly at their packs, them looking sneerily at our pale blue Lycra tights. So we hurried past in the heather.

At evening we looped back, and came on them again. They were peeling actual potatoes, and dropping them into solid aluminium pots. In a wide frying pan were chunks of dead chicken. United by tiredness, we stopped to chat. But the smell from the frying pan was, in the end, unbearable. Ahead of us was a meal of muesli and cold water, green glucose powder, and chewy bars. We made our excuses, hurried away into the evening, and attempted to enjoy it.

MIDGES ARE UNPLEASANT

Sometimes it's the little things that make all the difference. Especially if those little things are black, no more than 2mm long, and bite you. Midge is from the Norse *mygg*, which means mosquito. But midges are worse than mosquitoes because there are more of them. In Gaelic they're *Meanbh-chuileag*, which means 'very tiny fly'.

But we humans are cleverer than the insects. We can use tactics on them, and timing. If you walk before the middle of May, or after the middle of September, they will be lurking in the moss in their harmless larval form. In June they are bearable, or almost bearable. It's in the holiday months of July and August that they are at their worst.

The top speed of a midge is 2mph, or 3kmph; most of us humans can manage faster than that. It's when you stop moving that they start to gather. They home in on the CO_2 you breathe out, and on excited pheromones emitted by other midges. This means that the number of midges arriving at your skin surface increases as the square of the time you've been sitting. After five minutes – as you get your boots and socks off, and hunt down the blister plasters – the midges arriving are few and bearable. After twice as long, there will be four times as many – and you forget about plastering the blisters and struggle to get your socks back on while using both hands to beat away insects.

However, you don't need to keep moving so long as the air itself is moving past you. Even a slight breeze will keep the midges away.

When it comes to camping time, you're looking for somewhere low-level and sheltered in case the wind gets up. But if the evening is calm and still, reverse this. Seek somewhere up the mountainside, with breeze to keep away the insects. Occasionally the evening will be so calm and still that 'well up the mountainside' will be above the summits. I have been bitten by midges on Angel's Peak, the UK's fifth-highest mountain. But midges aren't all that interested in Munro-bagging, and there weren't very many of them up there.

Finally there are the physical defences. Before the trip, check the tent's midge defences. Even in the best-protected tent, you'll bring some midges in with you. Lying in the sleeping bag, gazing up at the tent roof and killing midges – just think, you could have been at home, on a comfortable sofa, operating the remote.

For evening wear around the camp, or for people in bivvy bags, there are various repellents – the ones made of herbs are less effective than those made of vicious chemicals. But I use a midge net. One night in the Cairngorms there were so many midges that I could actually hear a faint hum, the combined beating of thousands of tiny wings. And I was in a bivvy bag. But I was safe inside my midge net.

Keep the midge net in a tough little bag. Otherwise something in your rucksack will poke a hole in it.

MAY IS THE MONTH

There are two good times for long walks in Scotland, and one of them is the month of May. It rains less often in this month than in most others. The air is cool and clear: May photos are much better than those of hazy high summer. Sometimes the tops still carry a little snow, for high-altitude adventures if you want them or else for even more compelling camera-work. The morning chill gets you going: the evening is almost warm enough for a dip in the river. And the midges, as mentioned, are bearable or even absent.

Descending north from Beinn Chorranach, Ben Lui group ahead (Route 19)

The other good time – for sudden trips of two or three days – is any time at all. Weather forecasts are now available for up to seven days ahead. If the weather forecast suggests four days of mostly sunshine coming up, the one thing we know for sure is that it's going to pour down, from dawn on the first of those four days, to ten minutes after dusk on Day 4, ho-ho. However, if we can bring ourselves to be hopelessly naïve and actually believe the forecast, we'll find they got it right. Or near enough right to make it worthwhile packing our rucksack, getting a refund on the tickets for Glyndebourne, and heading impulsively into the hills.

Catch the good weather between the autumn storms, and autumn is every bit as walkable as spring, with the golden bonus of the autumn birch leaves. A midwinter sunny spell brings its own challenges. A down sleeping bag will keep you cosy under hard frost: but this makes it even more difficult getting out of it again, in the dark, and shaking the hoar frost off the inside of the tent. Frigid feet can still plod through the frost: the crucial trick is with the fingers, to get bootlaces tied, zips zipped, and a bearing set on the compass before they become stiff and incapable with the cold. But when 'Night's headtorch is burnt out, and jocund day Stands tiptoe on the misty mountain-tops', you don't have to be lying in bed with a naked Juliet (or Romeo, as appropriate). It's almost as much fun in your big boots, on a February morning in Glen Nevis.

PART 2 – BEGINNERISH BACKPACKING

SHOULDER-STRENGTHENING SHORT TRIPS

For any athletic endurance event, a schedule of training is crucial, plus the discipline to stick to it. But walking across Lochaber isn't an athletic event. It's meant to be a form of fun.

Probably you're doing a fair bit of fellwalking anyway. That will toughen up your feet, and the feet are fundamental. But if you suddenly put on a 12kg rucksack and then walk all day underneath it, your shoulders will suffer. There are muscles holding up that rucksack that have never had to hold anything more massive than your Margaret Thatcher-style shoulder pads.

A day walk rucksack weighs about 5kg; and you're used to that. What's useful is to then go for an all-day walk with a sack that's midway between 5kg (used-to-it) and 12kg (unbearable). An 8kg sack might contain a bivvy bag and sleeping bag, for a sleep-out on some favoured hill. That 8kg load will be bearable, or almost bearable, but will still bring those supine muscles into action. A fortnight later, the 12kg sack will be less of a shock to the shoulders.

THE OFF-ROUTE FOOD-FETCHING FORMULA

I'd planned myself a full coast-to-coast crossing, from Loch Shiel through to Aberdeenshire. It was just before I started that I realised that, for the first six days of the route (and more than halfway across Scotland) I hadn't given myself anywhere at all to go shopping…

Trouble was, those six days were over a score of mountains, not one of

Camp in Coire an Lochain, just below Ben Lui summit

which I'd been over before, and not one of which I was willing to not go over now. There were six of the shaggy Corbetts of Moidart and Ardgour, with birch-tree gorges in their sides and untrodden knolly ridges along their tops. There were the two Corryhully Munros. There was steep-sided Streap, the shapeliest non-Munro summit in the west. There were the three Corbetts all called Carn Dearg, or 'reddish stonepile'; three Deargs in a day, compelling. But even more compelling was to cover the entirety of Munro's Section 9. Section 9 is cited as the most boring section of them all. To get all nine of Section 9 done and out of the way, possibly also in a single day: obligatory.

Four days into the walk, there was a chance to walk out to Spean Bridge to resupply. The diversion, out and back, would be an extra six miles, all of it uninteresting. Was it worth it?

For these occasions I have a formula. A carry-day is one day's food carried for one day. It's worth walking one mile to save one carry-day of supplies. In the example above, if not stopping for shopping, I would be carrying 6 days' food the first day (6 carry-days), 5 days food the second day (5 carry-days), and so on. The total comes to 21 carry-days. Alternatively, between the coast and Spean Bridge, I'd be carrying 4 days food the first day, reducing to one day's food on the fourth day: 10 carry-days. Over the two following days to Kincraig on the Spey, I'd be carrying 2+1 = 3 carry-days. The total is 13 carry-days; a saving of 8 carry-days.

According to the formula, it's worth walking 8 miles extra to save those 8 carry-days; so I went to Spean Bridge. As a bonus, I got a hot lunch at the hotel.

STUFF, STUFFSACKS, AND THROWING IT ALL AWAY

I cannot go as fast as I would, by reason of this burden that is on my back.
Christian, in Pilgrim's Progress John Bunyan (1678)

When I reached the village of Soka in the evening, my bony shoulders were sore because of the load I had carried, which consisted of a paper coat to keep me warm at night, a light cotton gown to wear after the bath, scanty protection against the rain, writing equipment, and gifts from certain friends of mine. I wanted to travel light, of course, but there were always certain things I could not throw away.
Narrow Road to the Deep North Basho (1689)

Once I had mountains in the palm of my hand,
And rivers that ran through ev'ry day.
I must have been mad,
I never knew what I had,
Until I threw it all away.
Bob Dylan (1969)

Looking north from Lairig Dhoireann (Route 19)

Along comes the earthquake, or the forest fire: and that's when you whip out the handy multi-function self-rescue tool. Or else you don't, because you've got so much other stuff in your stuffsack that you can't lay hand on the danged thing.

'Lay not up for yourself treasures upon earth,' says the Bible. This applies even more when you have to put those earthly treasures in your rucksack and carry them for seven hours up Glen Etive. Christian, in John Bunyan's long-distance hiking epic *Pilgrim's Progress*, was relieved when his backpack fell off and rolled away on Mount Calvary. The burden of sin is heavy, but two spare fleeces and a sleeping bag liner can be almost as bad.

That said, there are all sorts of useful small items that really don't weigh all that much. The gas-powered tent lantern: people who carry one of those find it really useful. This is because people who carry stuff like gas-powered tent lanterns have such heavy packs that they don't get the tent up until long after sunset.

It's amazing what you can leave behind. One man on the John Muir Trail carried no food and survived by living off the land (that is, by scrounging off the rest of us). 'People carry far too much food,' he told me, 'it weighs them down. I'm doing them a big favour eating it for them.'

My fellrunning friend carries no sleeping bag. He puts on all his spare clothes and his waterproofs, and lies down on the groundsheet of the tent. Well, he would if he carried a tent. He actually carries a plastic fertiliser bag.

BACKPACK FACTS

Buachaille Etive Mor from the track to Black Corries Lodge (Route 21)

- **Start early** One hour from getting up to getting away is good. Two hours is poor. Maybe you're casual about getting in to work of a weekday; don't care if you do catch the later train in. But this is no commuter journey. This is backpacking and it's serious.
- **Stop early** There are important evening tasks like relaxing and paddling in the stream. Even ordinary stuff like cooking and unpacking the dry socks gets harder in the dark. Anyway, why waste batteries messing around under the moon? Sleep instead: you've an early start tomorrow…
- **Pack tidy** They tell us that no directory (or folder) on the computer should contain more than 20 items. If it does, put some of the items in a subdirectory. For rucksacks, the maximum number should be ten. Put small items in a special sub-sack for small items, evening items in a sub-sack for evening items. Is it nerdy to colour-code the sub-sacks? Yes it is, but do it anyway. And in the tent, everything should have its proper place. Did you think you'd come on holiday to get away from the housework? You were wrong.
- **Pick light** You deserve the best and most expensive of lightweight outdoor gear. The budget stuff is made of thinner material and lacks all sorts of important add-ons. So it actually weighs 500g less. Save your shame by cutting off the budget-brand labels: and save a few more grams as well.

↑ The tent you want is robust yet lightweight, stays up when it's windy, and doesn't cost more than you can afford. No tent has all these qualities. This simple single-skin tent weighs 1.8kg (rather heavy) and wasn't terribly expensive. It's easy it is to put up – 1 bendy pole and 5 pegs. Being single-skin with no through-draught, it's damp inside whatever the weather.

↓ Creise, and a budget tent – maybe even suitable for a music festival. This one is light – probably lighter than a more robustly built top-end tent. It's quite well designed for wind. It will wear out quite quickly, and this is just another of its advantages. You now know exactly what you need, and are ready to trade up to a slightly more expensive tent.

NOT THE WEST HIGHLAND WAY: A MOUNTAIN HIGH WAY

↑ *Lightweight and inexpensive: a two-person tarp weighing 500g. Not so much a tent, more of a 'sleeping tool': it is ingenious and adaptable (and its user has to be the same). The tent poles are trees or walking poles. Lumps of granite prop up the guy lines to increase indoor space and ventilation. In case of wind or snow, the walking pole is shortened and the guy lines are moved underneath the granite lumps, bringing the tent walls down against the ground. Note, though, that the surrounding scenery is not Scotland. For the benign climate and long, long distances of California's John Muir Trail the tarp tent served well. On a Scottish night of midges and drizzle it will be less satisfactory. (Especially if you never quite worked out how to make it stay up in the first place.)*

→ *Sandwood Bay, and a two-person, or 'one-and-a-half-person', tent from the 1980s of stout British manufacture. At 1.6kg it's reasonably light; with its three flexible poles threaded into the fabric it's reasonably easy to erect. In driving sleet half way up Ben Nevis, its seams leaked. The seams were resealed and, with a reproofing treatment every decade or so, it's been fine ever since. Its owner can't make any helpful comparisons with the expensive high-tech tents of today. He's never felt any urge to replace this one.*

NOT THE WEST HIGHLAND WAY: A MOUNTAIN HIGH WAY

↑ Lightweight, inexpensive and superbly designed: here is the one being used by a gear reviewer for TGO magazine on Beinn nan Aighenan, above Glen Kinglass (Route 16). It is robust, easy to pitch and windproof. It is large enough to share with an intimate companion, if not with a mere acquaintance. Without a groundsheet, it weighs 900gm. The inner has mesh at both ends, which solves the condensation problem, but makes it less cosy than it could be – and in storms you put your pack at the upwind end to receive the rain. The gear guru describes it as 'the best shelter design I've ever come across' and hates testing other tents because it stops him from sleeping in this one. And if you've walked far enough, you don't mind the damp and general discomfort.

→ The author's preferred shelter solution, especially when walking alone. The bivvy bag is cheap, light, and takes ten seconds to deploy. It won't blow down because it isn't up to start with; you never lose the pegs because there aren't any. On a nice night, like this one high on Stob Ghabhar (Route 10) you leave your face out under the stars. On a nasty night, though, the comfort level is too low for most people.

↑ A really well designed tent won't be as light as you'd like it to be, and it won't be cheap. But it's robust and won't tear apart on any sharp stones, and its low, curved shape will stay up in all but the very worst of storms. Its inner will zip up so's to be insect-proof, while its outer allows airflow to carry away the condensation. Just make sure you've worked out how those complicated poles go in before you pack it up for its first hike. This one's at Grisedale Tarn in the Lake District.

Steall Falls in autumn, in the rain

NOT THE WEST HIGHLAND WAY: A MOUNTAIN HIGH WAY

ROUTE 15
A mostly gentle two-day: the back of Ben Nevis

Start	Kings House
Finish	Fort William Station
Distance	50km (31 miles)
Ascent	800m (2700ft)
Approximate time	14hr (two days)
Maximum altitude	550m Devil's Staircase; 400m Loch Eilde Mor
Terrain	Tracks and paths – mostly good, but rough along Abhainn Rath and upper Water of Nevis
Facilities	
Kings House (start)	Citylink coaches, hotel with bunkhouse
Kinlochleven	All facilities
Abhainn Rath	Bothy (Meanach)
Glen Nevis	Youth hostel and bunkhouse (Ben Nevis Inn)
Fort William	Trains and Citylink coaches, all facilities

'Is it very long?' Alice asked, for she had heard a good deal of poetry that day.
'It's long, but it's very, very beautiful. Everybody that hears me sing it — either it brings tears to their eyes, or else —'
'Or else what?' said Alice, for the Knight had made a sudden pause.
'Or else it doesn't, you know.'
Alice in Wonderland Lewis Carroll (1865); the White Knight's song parodies a well-known long-distance walker, William Wordsworth.

You could start this from Kinlochleven, as a robust alternative to the West Highland Way. It may well bring tears to your eyes; it is certainly very, very beautiful. The Kinlochleven start brings it down to just 36km (22 miles) with 450m (1500ft) of total ascent (about 10hr walking time). If you finish at Glen Nevis Youth Hostel, that's 4km shorter still. So this works as a rough, romantic and rather strenuous final day for the West Highland Way.

When considered as a walk in its own right, Kings House is easier to get to, and makes the route into a good two-day length. After a 15km warm-up along the West Highland Way, Kinlochleven becomes a resupply point for

ROUTE 15 – A MOSTLY GENTLE TWO-DAY: THE BACK OF BEN NEVIS

everything you now realise you should have brought along. It also has handy litter bins for all those little luxuries now reclassified as burdensome junk.

From Kinlochleven, the way is a reasonably easy walk through big, serious country. The start and end are beautiful, on smooth tracks or firm stony paths. The bit in the middle is bleaker. But in the middle of the bleak bit is the perfectly placed bothy of Meanach (extended by the Ordnance Survey to Meannanach). It may not be nearly so nice as a tent at the riverside, but it's there if that riverside tent collapses.

To complete the symmetry, there's a waterfall at the edge of Kinlochleven; another one, the Steall Falls, at the end of the wild bit. Lower Glen Nevis requires you to ignore the tarmac road and enjoy the path on the other side of the river. But for the blistered and miserable, that road does have a bus service along it.

Kings House is on the Citylink direct coach route from Glasgow. You could arrive at lunchtime, enjoy a hot lunch, and set out for Kinlochleven. Or you could arrive in the evening and have a hot supper; then camp alongside the River Etive (permitted but slightly squalid informal camping) and get a hot breakfast as well.

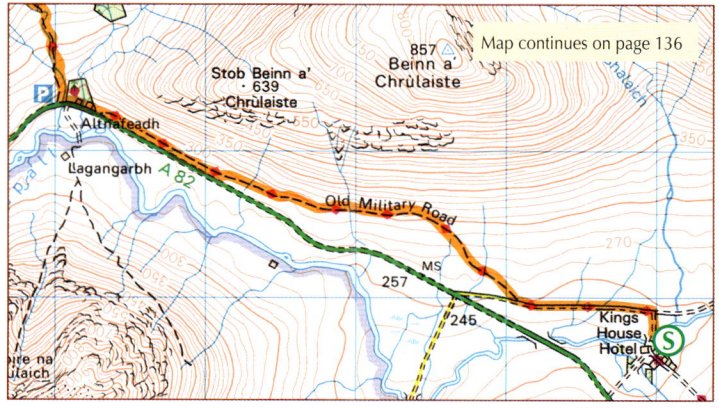

Cross the bridge alongside the hotel and follow the small, old road westwards. After 1km the WH Way turns up right, on the path of the old military road. After 3km it runs alongside the A82 past Altnafeadh, then turns steeply uphill and crosses the Devil's Staircase to Kinlochleven. For more details see 'Kings House to Kinlochleven' in Part 1. Kings House to Kinlochleven 13km (8 miles), about 4.5hr.

NOT THE WEST HIGHLAND WAY: A MOUNTAIN HIGH WAY

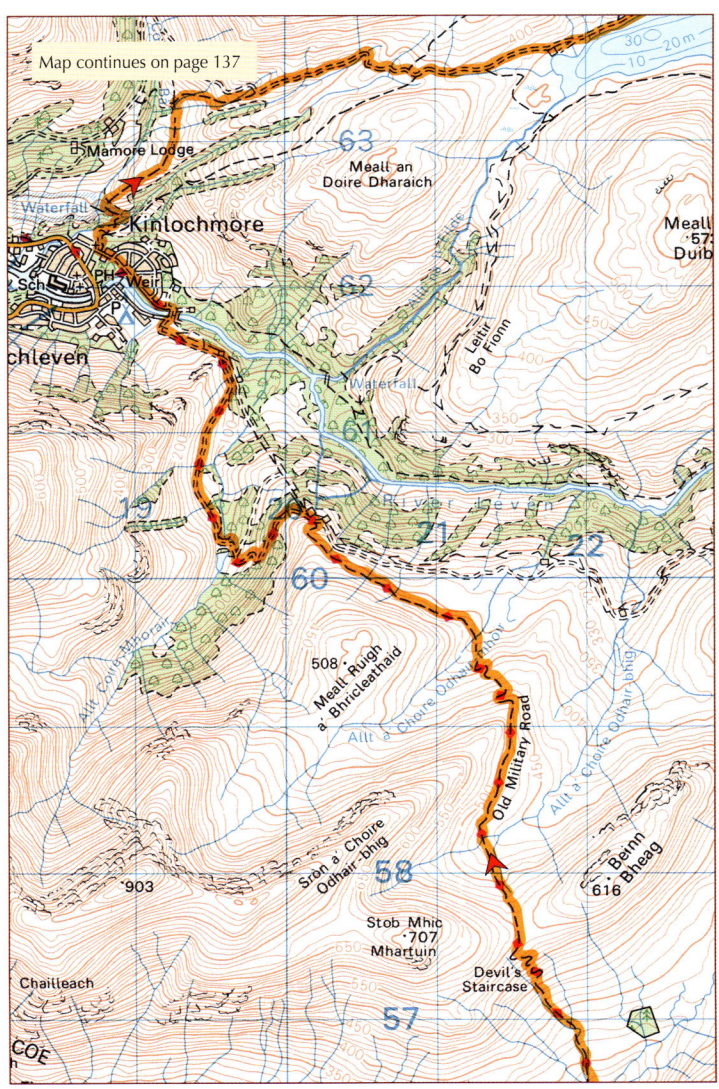

Route 15 – A mostly gentle two-day: the back of Ben Nevis

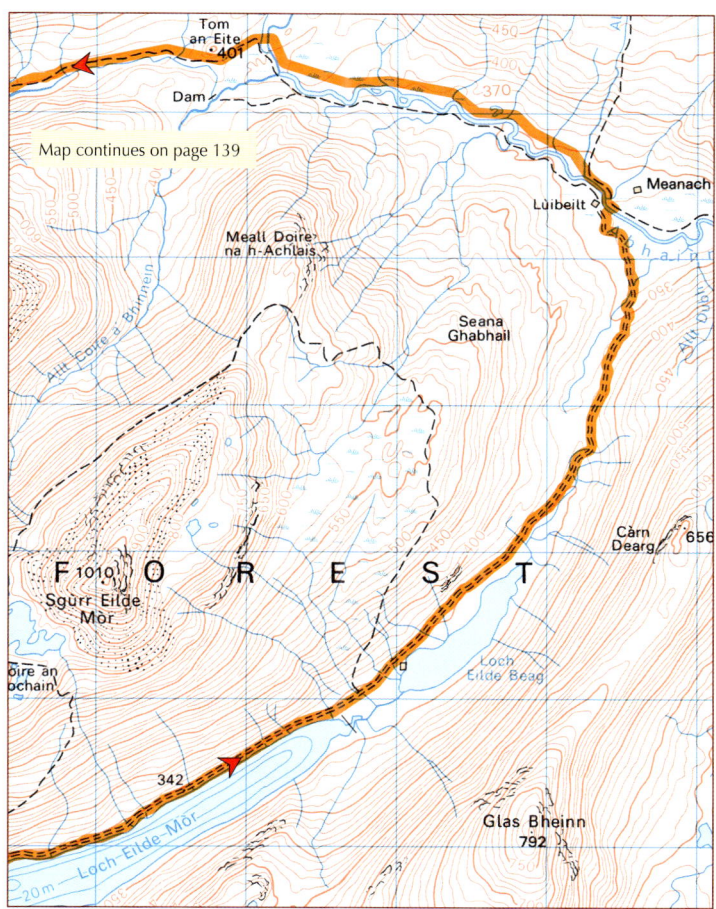

Map continues on page 139

From the **Grey Mare's car park** in Wade Road, the best way to the high track is by the yellow-arrowed trail – the red-arrow one is shorter but eroded and less pretty. Behind the car park turn left on the main trail. After a first glimpse of the waterfall comes a descent to cross a footbridge. The waterfall is now 100 metres away to the left.

Not the West Highland Way: A Mountain High Way

In Glen Nevis, below Aonach Beag

After visiting the Grey Mare's Waterfall, return to take the stony path uphill. It's steep, and it's rough, and it's tough. But cheer up, just look at the wonderful view along Loch Leven! That doesn't work? Well, the tough bit is over in half an hour, and there won't be anything else like that afterwards, promise. For the path eases off to a junction, where the green/yellow trail forks up to the right. After a gate in a deer fence, it runs along the left side of a spur, across two streams, to another path junction. Here the yellow arrow points up to the right, to pass out through the deer fence again and reach a broad smooth track with fabulous views.

Turn right and follow this track right through the mountains passing (count them) not one but two lovely lakes – **Loch Eilde Mòr** and **Loch Eilde Beag**. The track ends at the ruins of **Luibeilt**. Kinlochleven to Luibeilt 11.5km (7 miles), about 4hr.

In normal summer conditions you can cross the river here, to the bothy at **Meanach**. If the river is in spate, you'll have to stay south of it – there are rough

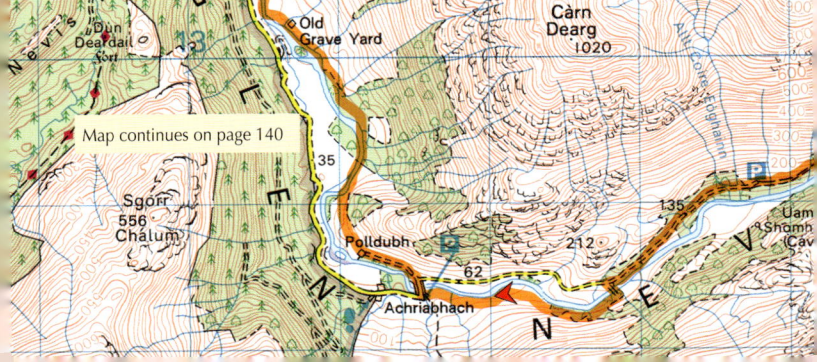

ROUTE 15 – A MOSTLY GENTLE TWO-DAY: THE BACK OF BEN NEVIS

Meanach (or Meannanach) bothy, at the top end of Glen Nevis

paths on both banks. Head upstream, until the stream, now small, turns up to the north.

If you crossed to the north bank, you must now recross it, but this is not difficult. Head west for 200 metres, passing across the saddle point to a hummock called **Tom an Eite**. The path runs immediately to left of this, to follow the right bank of the small stream running down beyond. The path stays to right of the stream, and gets gradually better; the stream gets bigger and becomes the **Water of Nevis**.

After 5km the path crosses a sidestream by a footbridge beside the ruined remains of Steall. Now the well-used path passes along a meadow opposite the enormous **Steall Waterfall**. You could cross the so-called footbridge of three steel cables to visit the waterfall's base. But the main path continues to right of the river, through woods along the steep side of the Nevis Gorge, to a car park at the top of the **Glen Nevis** road.

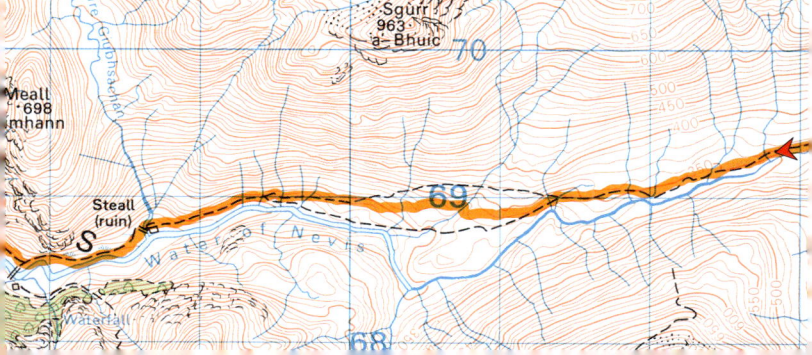

NOT THE WEST HIGHLAND WAY: A MOUNTAIN HIGH WAY

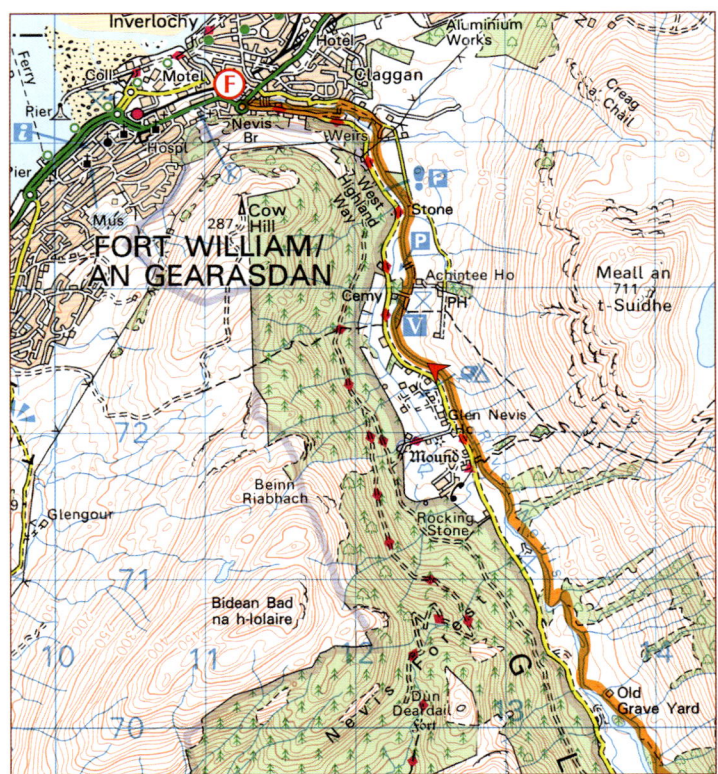

Look miserable, and you might hitch a lift despite the big wet rucksack. Otherwise, head down the road for 1.5km to cross a footbridge down left. Continue to left of the river to the lower waterfalls near **Polldubh**. More detail of the Glen Nevis path in Route 12.

There are buses to Fort William from here, but better is to turn briefly right, up-valley, to cross the road bridge above the waterfalls, then take a track on the left, which leads to Polldubh cottage; and then the rough but very pretty path to right of River Nevis all the way to Fort William. Stride into the Nevisport Bar, plonk your wet rucksack onto the floor, and demand beer. Luibeilt to Fort William 22km (13½ miles), about 5.5hr.

ROUTE 16
A wilder two-day: Taynuilt to Bridge of Orchy

Start	Taynuilt
Finish	Bridge of Orchy
Distance	40km (25 miles)
Ascent	400m (1300ft)
Approximate time	11hr (1½ days)
Maximum altitude	Pass above Loch Dochard 290m
Terrain	Smooth track until Glenkinglass Lodge; rougher track and some wet paths to finish
Facilities	
Taynuilt (start)	Citylink coaches (Oban route) and trains; hotel and small shop
Glen Kinglass	Narrachan bothy
Loch Dochard	Very small and basic stable shelter
Inveroran	Hotel
Bridge of Orchy (end)	Trains and Citylink coaches; hotel with bunkhouse, independent hostel on station

This route is more serious than the previous one, as there's no resupply point and no convenient escape until you get through to Inveroran. However, the going is gentle, on smooth tracks built for estate vehicles. One young aristocrat impressed a future father-in-law by driving all the way to Glenkinglass Lodge in his powder-blue Rolls Royce.

Once the Rollers have turned off, the track gets rougher to pass Loch Dochard. Over the last part of the walk you'll dip your feet in the peat, as 2km of the path passes through a swamp.

Head north through **Taynuilt** village across River Nant. At a church, turn right on a street through **Brochroy**. It becomes a track, where you fork left past the Bonawe Furnace (worth a visit). Move onto a parallel track on the right, through woods. Where it bends right towards the A85, turn left to cross an impressive footbridge over **River Awe**.

Cross a field to the car park of Inverawe Country Park. Turn right on a back road for 700 metres, then left up a forest track (tarmac to start with). The main track leads northeast through woods above Loch Etive. It runs down to the lochside, then turns inland a little to cross River Noe.

Not the West Highland Way: A Mountain High Way

Taynuilt

Keep ahead on the main track past **Glennoe Farm**. The track is tarred at its high corner, and runs along the steep face above Loch Etive rather thrillingly. (Even more so in one's powder-blue Rolls Royce.) It drops under oaks to a bridge over euphonious River Liver, rises again across open moor, then drops to cross a fine bridge at Inverkinglass near **Ardmaddy**.

Just after this bridge keep right on the track up **Glen Kinglass**. The track is well surfaced for estate vehicles, but on the right and nearer the river are remnants of an old track which is pleasanter to walk on. The glen is open, but overlooked by craggy slopes, on some of which natural woods of birch and pine are being encouraged. After 3km, over on the left is the estate hut called Narrachan which has in the past been available for bothy use.

Not the West Highland Way: A Mountain High Way

Loch Etive track from Taynuilt

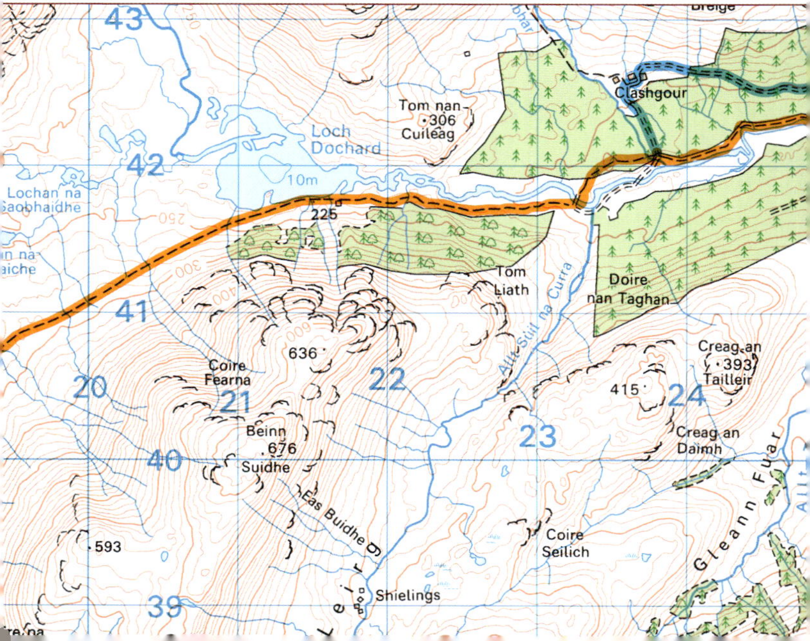

Route 16 – A wilder two-day: Taynuilt to Bridge of Orchy

After 10km of easy walking up the glen, the track approaches **Glenkinglass Lodge**. Taynuilt to Glenkinglass Lodge 22.5km (14 miles), about 5.5hr.

As the track bends right towards the lodge, keep ahead on a rough old track, surfaced with granite cobbles, still to left of the main river. It fords a sidestream, with a footbridge alongside, then joins the main river.

After 2km turn down right to a new bridge not marked on maps (NN 1857 3991), then turn left, upstream along the riverbank. After 400 metres pass a disused and partly dismantled footbridge, to rejoin the rough track at its ford alongside.

Continue along the track, which is here little used, and hard to spot as it crosses some bare granite. It leads through a high, wild pass to **Loch Dochard**. At the trackside, Loch Dochard stable has a roof but no windows, and a cobbled floor. It offers uncomfortable emergency shelter. Glenkinglass Lodge to Loch Dochard 6.5km (4 miles), about 2.5hr.

In another 1.5km a footbridge on the left leads to a marshy path. It crosses a ladder stile then runs along a soggy forest clearing to a stream crossing below Clashgour. The former bridge here has been removed. If the ford is too full, you'll have to struggle up the near bank to a bridge above Clashgour. Otherwise, you could cross to a track up to Clashgour and turn right on its gently descending access track – this goes through a gate to rejoin the river. However, unless you're

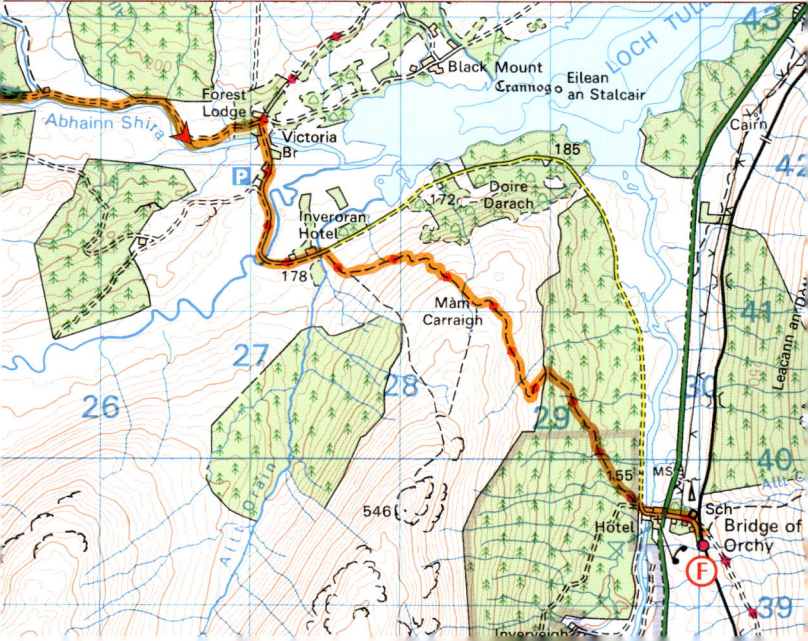

NOT THE WEST HIGHLAND WAY: A MOUNTAIN HIGH WAY

very tired, it is better to take a grassy, fairly dry path along the main Abhainn Shira riverbank to join the track arriving from Clashgour.

The track runs downstream to **Forest Lodge**. Turn right along the road across **Victoria Bridge** (with a fine view back up Glen Shira). A second bridge has informal roadside camping, before Inveroran Hotel (inexpensive B&B, good bar meals).

Just past the hotel the well-made WH Way path turns up to the right. It ascends to a viewpoint cairn, then drops gradually along the line of the old military road. After a zigzag it enters forest, to reach the road beside the bridge at **Bridge of Orchy**. There's informal camping on the near side of the river. Bridge of Orchy itself has a hotel and an independent hostel on the station; trains and buses; but no shop. Loch Dochard to Bridge of Orchy 11km (7 miles), about 3hr.

Bridge of Orchy Hotel

PART THREE
Away from the Way

Descending from Ben Lui towards the col for Beinn a' Chleibh

Across Rannoch Moor from A' Chruach (Route 21); the distant hill is Schiehallion

Every walk starts off with an idea: and the idea of the West Highland Way is a good one. Start at the Lowland edge, and walk northwards for the inside of a week, by glens and lochs, woodland and mountain passes; and when you get to the Great Glen, stop.

The idea of the West Highland Way is such a good one that it's wasted on the West Highland Way. There are even better ways than that converted old road as it hugs its narrow strip of civilisation (if civilisation is the correct term for what Fort William Chamber of Commerce calls the 'A82 corridor').

So here are some more committing and serious departures from the WH Way. These routes don't return to the official way even for the overnight stops. They head north in the empty glens, or over the mountains, or along lonely Loch Etive where the peat froth hits the seaweed.

The WH Way could have started in the heart of Glasgow: that's a nice idea but a fairly nasty walk. But maybe it should have started at the sea? It seemed a bit too radical to depart from the WH Way before it had even started. So I put the day walk out of Dumbarton, over the Kilpatrick Hills, in this section instead of in Part One.

Once in the Highlands, there's another alternative start point: this time at Arrochar, on the wrong side of Loch Lomond. A day through (or over) the Arrochar Alps brings you

PART 3 – AWAY FROM THE WAY

into contact with the WH Way at Inverarnan. But at once, Route 19 darts off sideways for a full crossing of Ben Lui and the long walk up the side of Loch Etive.

After crossing the Devil's Staircase to Kinlochleven, the next of the parallel walks heads off northeast for Loch Treig and the high gap of the Lairig Leacach. Having affronted the WH Way by not starting at Milngavie, you add further insult by finishing at Spean Bridge. And at Route 21 a more austere side-path heads east from Kings House to taste the real remoteness of Rannoch Moor.

Detailed OS map extracts for these routes would have made this book bulky and unsuitable for a backpack. More importantly, they wouldn't have been the clearest way of tracing these rambling lines. Instead, the overview maps at the beginning of this book show how these various aberrant ways intertwine with the established WH Way, the hill alternatives of Part One, and the two beginner backpacks of Part Two.

Lairig Leacach (Route 20)

Not the West Highland Way: A Mountain High Way

ROUTE 17
Dumbarton Start

Start	Dumbarton Castle Rock
Finish	Drymen
Distance	30.5km (19 miles)
Ascent	650m (2200ft)
Approximate time	9hr
Maximum altitude	Duncolm 401m
Terrain	Paths and pathless grassy hillsides, with two patches of rougher tussocks
Facilities	
Dumbarton (start)	The railway station is Dumbarton East. Car parking at the foot of the castle (may be full when Dumbarton are playing at home).
Dumgoyne	Glengoyne Distillery, Beech Tree Inn
Drymen (end)	All facilities

Dumbarton is where it should have started. Like Milngavie it has a convenient railway station; unlike Milngavie it has a magnificent castle as well. Milngavie ejects you from the city edge into country parkland, but Dumbarton kicks you straight into the hills. And the Clyde is tidal, like Loch Linnhe; so done from Dumbarton the West Highland Way becomes a true coast-to-coast (albeit the west coast both times!).

The Kilpatrick Hills, oddly enough, stood in for Rourke's Drift in the 'Zulu' sequence of Monty Python's *The Meaning of Life*. 'Get some walking in, and try and live together in peace and harmony with people of all creeds and nations': this is the Meaning of Life, according to Monty Python. It's hard to argue with that, or to imagine a more southerly start, for a walk to Fort William, than the other end of Africa.

If you find the right way, those film-star Kilpatricks give you pleasant grass to wander along, the small but sudden Duncolm, great views northwards to Loch Lomond, and an equally interesting view south to the mist-shrouded skyscrapers of Glasgow.

ROUTE 17 – DUMBARTON START

If you find the wrong way, the Kilpatricks give you a serious aerobic workout, followed by a gritted-up filter on your washing machine. The first time I crossed the Kilpatricks was at night. Steering from tussock to tussock with the compass and torch and moonlight on the reservoirs: it was an interesting experience, but not one I want to repeat. The Earl of Argyll had a similar trip in 1685. Unwisely deciding to march his army across in the dark, he got to Old Kilpatrick to find he'd only 500 men left – the others had given up and gone home.

Those Campbell chieftains might have been better sticking to the regular West Highland Way. Forty years before, Argyll's father had been defeated at Fort William when his enemy Montrose used Route 20 (later in this section) to bypass his army…However, it's not necessary to suffer Campbell-style across the Kilpatricks. There are grassy pathways above the swamps; all you do is link them together and not get lost. Then just enjoy the wide view of Clyde, the woodland paths, and the small green hills. Plus, as a surprise bonus, Scotland's slot canyon at the Whangie.

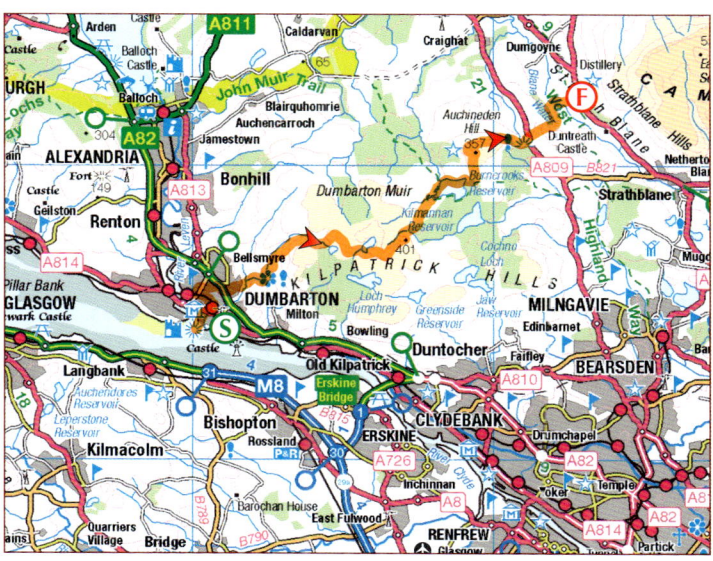

Dumbarton Rock

From Dumbarton Castle take the street inland past Dumbarton football ground. You can then short-cut by slanting diagonally right across Knoxland Square. Reach the Glasgow Road (A814) and turn right, under the railway and past **Dumbarton East Station**. At once turn left into green space with playing fields.

Head up the right-hand edge of the playing fields, next to Gruggie's Burn, to a tarmac cycle path. Turn right for 50 metres, then left into unsurfaced Silvertonhill Lane. Keep ahead (northeast) through Silverton to the A82 dual carriageway.

Turn left, crossing the busy dual carriageway as convenient. Pass the **Police HQ**, and at once turn right through a substantial stone gateway. Keep ahead into a tarred pathway uphill. This crosses a residential street, between stone gateposts into the grounds of Overtoun House. Keep uphill on a track until it steepens, where a path down into the woods on the right is signed as 'woodland path diversion'.

Take the path upstream on the wooded bank above Overtoun Burn. After a small footbridge bear right to stay above the main stream, soon passing a waterfall on the other side (Spardie Linn, heard but in summer not seen). The path crosses the burn and heads along the top of the burn bank, now to right of the burn as it passes **Overtoun House**.

Turn left over the high stone bridge, then take a path on the right, upstream. Ignore a first footbridge on the right, then fork right to cross the second one. The path passes a vegetated pool, then forks. Bear up right to a path 'T'. Here you turn left to an old metal gate onto open pasture above the woods.

ROUTE 17 – DUMBARTON START

Slant up to the right to find a wide grass path. Follow this up the valley, with the burn down on your left and **Lang Craigs** up on the right. After a pleasant mile, the path bends up right, to a gate into a forest plantation, with a sign 'Crags Circular Path'. Don't enter the plantation, but turn down left, along the forest edge, to its corner. Here you cross a stream. If you 'dough not' want to visit Doughnot, you can continue directly uphill, to left of Black Linn reservoir then crossing a stream, onto Darnycaip above.

Head northeast up a grassy slope with bracken patches to the trig pillar on **Doughnot Hill**.

The flat plateau now lying to the southeast is a morass of tussocks and sphagnum moss. It resembles the muskeg of Arctic Canada and is just the sort of stuff that discouraged the tough Campbells. So head down a rough path southeast (unless you're an even tougher MacDonald with something to prove, when you'll just plunge east into the tussocks).

That rough path leads along the bottom edge of the tussock prairie, towards Darnycaip (the minor summit above Black Linn Reservoir). No need to visit it, just turn northeast along a grassy/heathery ridgeline above the tussock swamp. A small path heads northeast along the ridgeline, to reach Fyn Loch just to left of its dam.

Cross the dam and follow the loch shore around its southern corner. Here join a grassy quad-bike trail running up onto **Fynloch Hill**. Fynloch has a 400m contour ring on the Explorer map, so could overtop 401m Duncolm and be the summit of the Kilpatricks. Let's hope not: Duncolm is far finer than Fynloch.

Doughnot Hill to the Clyde

Descend southeast, to the col between Fynloch Hill and Little Duncolm. Aim for a small hummock standing in the col to find a quad-bike path down to the left. It runs along the northern flank of Middle Duncolm, with a drier path just above on the right, then reaches the base of Duncolm. The path spirals to the left to reach the summit of **Duncolm**. Duncolm: Dun (or fort) of St Columba. The Kilpatricks are formed of flat-topped basalt lava flows; the upstanding Duncolm and Dumbarton Rock are former volcanic vents plugged with hard, welded lava.

Descend the same path, until you can turn down to the right and spiral below Duncolm's northern crag to join a wall below. There's a wet path on the far side of the wall. Follow this northeast, soon with a clear-felled plantation on your right, crossing the outflow of Lily Loch. The grassy path continues to right (south) of the loch. Turn off it, north, to pass the loch head, and continue gently uphill for about 200 metres.

Now you can look down to **Burncrooks Reservoir**. There are low humps of smoother grass rising above the tussocks, and a small path can be found running down a succession of these humps. This path heads to the reservoir corner where Burn Crooks flows into it (NS 479 788). Cross the burn; now a wet peaty path crosses the moor to the reservoir dam – or if the water is low, walk along the reservoir shore.

Cross the dam to a smooth track. Follow this past the reservoir, then through a gate. Just before a cutting, turn off left. Two basalt crag lines slant left up Auchineden Hill. A small path runs up the terrace above the lower crag, before easing up to the right onto the main crest. It runs up to the trig on **Auchineden Hill**.

There is a path running straight down northeast, but this misses the whole point of this hill, which is the geological oddity on its west side. So take a different path sharp left, descending west into a grassy hollow. Ignore a side-path off to the right, but stay on the path down the hollow. At its foot the path bends right, to the base of a small crag.

At once there's a rock slot on the right. Take the path through this small slot canyon, **the Whangie**.

Pass along the slot, which briefly becomes a balcony with a view of Loch Lomond. At the slot end, you could turn down left past a spine-like pinnacle to visit the crags. However the path continues ahead, passing out onto open hill. This path contours forward around the flank of Auchineden Hill; it is well used and quite muddy and stony. After passing a defunct ladder stile, it runs downhill to a swamp, crossed on worn-out railway sleepers, and a wall stile into **Queens View car park**. Poor Queen! Even ignoring the foreground of tarmac and parked cars, this is the first point of the walk without a particularly interesting view.

From the car park exit cross the road and head north for 60 metres. Cross a low point in the roadside wall, to a trampled way through rushes northeast. After crossing a stream, get onto grassier ground rising towards the hummock of **Quinloch Muir top**. Skirt to left of this top, to the broad, rush-choked col to its north.

WHAT IS THE WHANGIE?

The Whangie pinnacle

There are three theories. It could be a slash-mark left by the Devil's tail. It could be glacial plucking: ice gripped the cliff face then moved inexorably downhill, pulling the front slab of rock with it. Or it could be a meltwater channel: a stream obstructed by the glacier from flowing downhill, so carving out a gorge sideways.

As you pass along the slot, look at its sides. At one point, the shapes of the two sides visibly match up. This suggests that it was pulled apart, rather than gouged out by water or the Satanic backside. Also, the pinnacle just to left of the exit looks to have been similarly snatched, just slightly further downhill.

Just to north now is the fort on Quinlochmore, with an earthwork running through the col northwards. Leave this on your left, as you descend northeast to a gate between two woods (Quinloch Wood and South Wood). Go down between the woods, and under a power pylon line.

At the slope foot, follow a track to the left. It runs along the foot of Quinloch Wood then behind the buildings of **Quinloch**, where it bends right to become the driveway. It crosses Strath Blane's floor and a small stream, then crosses the **WH Way**.

Turn left for 10km (6 miles, about 2.5hr) to **Drymen**.

NOT THE WEST HIGHLAND WAY: A MOUNTAIN HIGH WAY

ROUTE 18
Wrong side of the loch: the Arrochar Alps

Start	Arrochar & Tarbet Station
Finish	Inverarnan
Distance	25km (15½ miles)
Ascent	1550m (5000ft)
Approximate time	9.5hr
Maximum altitude	Ben Ime 1011m
Terrain	Mountain paths, grassy ridges. vehicle track and a rough woodland descent
Facilities	
Tarbet on Loch Lomond (start)	Trains and Citylink coaches, occasional Loch Lomond ferry from Rowardennan; hotel
Arrochar	Shops, café and hotels
Inveruglas	Citylink coaches, Loch Lomond ferries to Inversnaid; café
Inverarnan (end)	Citylink coaches; nearest station Ardlui (3km of WH Way then ferry from Ardleish); Drover's Inn, Beinglas campsite with café and shop

If taking a high wild route, why bother with the Lowlands? Start at Tarbet on the other bonnie bank of Loch Lomond, the western one, for a route through the Arrochar Alps to Inverarnan.

The Cobbler fails to reach the supposedly magical Munro altitude of 914.4m. Despite this – and quite rightly – it's one of the most popular hills in the Highlands. In its slightly smaller way, it is blessed with spectacular crags, and a north summit that hangs over the abyss. That north summit is actually quite easy, but the central one is the true top, and isn't easy at all. It's a small rock tower perched above the corrie. In dry calm conditions it's a slightly demoralising scramble. In the wet and wind it's serious.

But if, through weather or wimpishness, you don't attain those final 5m, that's just an excuse to come back another day to this delightful summit – perhaps with a reliable companion and a rope.

A well-worn Munro-baggers' path leads onto Ben Ime. But down the back is different. The ridge is grassy and well defined; but because it leads

ROUTE 18 – WRONG SIDE OF THE LOCH: THE ARROCHAR ALPS

to no road, it is entirely unpathed. This is the reward for walking in simple straight lines rather than up and down from car parks.

Some people, when it comes to wild mountain ground, get excited and like to overdo it a bit. For them there's a sideways diversion to take in Ben Vane as well.

A long track then leads out along Strath Dubh-uisge. The name means glen of dark waters: the gloom implied in the name is accentuated by the forestry plantations. However, the forest access tracks make for an easy walk out. Please note that the author surveyed the awkward descent to the A82 over 10 years ago now, and a better route may currently be available.

Now if the wildness has taken control of you, then leave the trodden Way again at once for the Ben Lui pass (Route 6) or the high way over the top of Lui towards Loch Etive (Route 19 following).

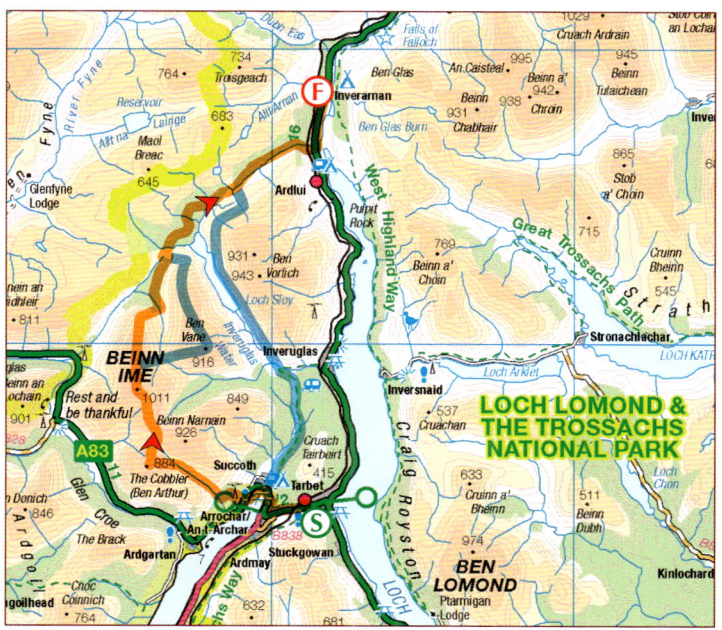

Not the West Highland Way: A Mountain High Way

Main route over Ben Ime

After the scenic and slightly surprising train ride up the Gareloch and Loch Long, alight at **Arrochar and Tarbet Station**. If arriving by coach at Tarbet on Loch Lomond, take the pavement of the A83 (signed Campbeltown) for 800 metres, and fork up right to the station.

Pass under the railway and turn left on a path through woods around the base of Cruach Tairbeirt. After 1.5km a path forks down left into **Arrochar** village (or the path ahead becomes the foul-weather alternative towards Inveruglas: see page 166).

Follow the main road around the head of Loch Long. Just past the second car park, a wide path forks up right for the Cobbler. Follow it up to a forest road, which it joins for 50 metres towards a mobile phone mast. The path continues uphill on the right, through scrubby birch trees, to reach open hill at 350m altitude near a reservoir on the **Allt a' Bhalachain** (Buttermilk Burn).

The well-made path runs uphill to right of the burn, passing the two large **Narnain Boulders**. In another 300 metres, a path turns off to the left, crossing the stream. It becomes a steep, bouldery mess as it climbs into the Cobbler's eastern corrie. However it improves somewhat for the final and steepest section, up below the overhang of the north peak to the col between the north peak and the Cobbler's higher central peak.

A brief trip up to the right over gentle slabs gains the **north peak**. Return across the col, and take the path up the right flank to the rounded gravel hilltop that seems to be the Cobbler's summit, but isn't, quite.

The true summit of **the Cobbler** is the neighbouring rock tower, the **Argyll Needle**. It is a scramble Grade 2, over rather smooth rock that becomes treacherous when damp. There is a serious drop below.

Loch Long, from the path to Arrochar

The summit of the Cobbler, with Ben Lomond seen in the distant view on the left

To reach that true top, approach the tower over boulders on its left, to pass through a short rock tunnel – the eye of the Argyll Needle. This brings you to a shelf on the Needle's exposed southern side. Walk along the shelf, and climb up a gentle ramp beyond, to a hollow below two perched boulders. Clamber onto these, and then back left to the small platform summit. Scramble down again the same way.

Descend back to the col between the central and north summits. Continue ahead on a path that contours the left side of the North Peak. It is well built, and descends northwards to a complex col between the Cobbler, Ben Narnain and Ben Ime.

Cobbler North Top

Follow the level path northwards, to a gate in a fence. From here the path ascends northwest up the broad slope of Ben Ime. It tends to disappear on the wide grassland, but as the ridge narrows the path reforms, leading just left of the final crest to **Ben Ime** summit. The trig point marked on maps has been shattered by lightning.

Head down the north slope, which forms a broadly rounded ridge. The right-hand side of the slope is cragged, so the small path edges left towards the slope rim (views of Beinn an Lochain) then slants down to the right into the ridge-foot col, Glas Bhealach. Here turn down right for the strenuous Ben Vane add-on.

Continue up the slope opposite to **Beinn Chorranach**; and then down its gentle north ridge. As it descends, the ridgeline gradually bends northeast. At its foot,

Back to Ben Ime, from Beinn Chorranach

ROUTE 18 – WRONG SIDE OF THE LOCH: THE ARROCHAR ALPS

grassy terraces between small outcrops lead down to a deer fence with a convenient ladder stile (NN 260 112, 50 metres to left of the high point of the fence). Rough, ungrazed grassland leads down to an intake dam, which you cross.

A covered leat (artificial stream) and a small track contour around the flank of Ben Ime above trees, north then northeast. After a deer-fence gate, the main track turns down left, to cross the floor of **Glen Kinglas** through a lower gate to a track junction. Arrochar & Tarbet to Glen Kinglas 15.5km (10 miles), 1450m (4900ft), about 7hr; the alternative route over Ben Vane rejoins here.

Turn right, soon through another gate into forest. The track climbs gently at first, and after 3km emerges into a strip of open ground. At a junction, take the track on the left back into trees. It runs down-valley, finally dropping towards the stream on its right, to end just above the valley's final downhill steepening. Recent maps show this track now continuing ahead, to zigzag back down to the A82 1km south of Inverarnan.

Cross the decomposing deer fence just below (there's a convenient hole in it), then the stream. The next pylon downhill is at the valley steepening and is the last one you can see. Take a quad-bike track under the wires down to this 'final' pylon. Here there starts a small indistinct path, bearing to right away from the wires. Keep a sharp eye on it, as if you lose it the descent will be uncomfortable.

The path runs under birch woods, and slants down southeast until directly above a house (a recently refurbished chapel) at the side of the A82. It then turns directly downhill towards this house. Reach the railway immediately to right of its bridge over the stream. Cross to a stile, and head down to left of the chapel to the A82.

Turn left along the busy road for almost 2km to **Inverarnan**. Glen Kinglas to Inverarnan 9.5km (5½ miles), about 2.5hr.

Not the West Highland Way: A Mountain High Way

Bonus peak: Ben Vane

Distance	25km (15½ miles): Arrochar - Ben Vane - Inverarnan
Ascent	1900m (6300ft)
Approximate time	10hr

Ben Vane is a fine upstanding summit, usually ascended as a straight up-and-down from the Loch Lomond side. The Lag Uaine, or 'green hollow', at its back is a wild place among high grass slopes and waterfalls, which feels more remote than it actually is. If you want to divide this route into two short days, it provides a natural campsite.

Follow the previous route over the Cobbler and Ben Ime to descend from Ben Ime to **Glas Bhealach**.

From the lowest point of the col descend gentle grassy slopes to the right (east). As the slope steepens, there's a small crag outcrop. If you find yourself at the top of this, move to the left to follow a stream down beside it. Keep straight downhill alongside the two streams below, which meet just above the wide col (**Lag Uaine**) between Beinn Ime and Ben Vane. Arrochar & Tarbet to Lag Uaine 11.5km (7 miles), 1300m (4300ft), about 5.5hr.

The Cobbler, from the slopes of Ben Ime

Route 18 – Wrong side of the loch: the Arrochar Alps

Loch Lomond and Ben Vane from Inveruglas

Head northeast across the wide col, and turn east up the slope of Ben Vane. Small but steep crags interrupt the lowest slope, and are bypassed on the left. Then just keep uphill. Eventually you'll reach **Ben Vane**'s summit plateau. The summit cairn lies beyond a small seasonal pool at the far edge of the plateau: in case of doubt, immediately behind the cairn, the east ridge path arrives up a notch in a small crag band.

From the summit return west to a cairn at the opposite end of the plateau, and head down northwest, with care in mist. At 700m a small lochan marks the beginning of the rambling north ridge. This has various short but steep ups and downs, confusing in mist, before the small cairn of **Beinn Dubh**.

Continue down north, with steeper drops to Loch Sloy to the right. At 375m altitude you'll pass under a power line (which at this point divides to carry its six cables on two, smaller, pylons of three cables each). Follow the cables down left to the corner of a track. This track has arrived from the left along a covered water-channel, and is the line of the main route above.

Follow it down ahead across the valley floor, through a gate, to a track junction; and continue as on the main route above to **Inverarnan**. Lag Uaine to Inverarnan 13.5km (8½ miles), 600m (2000ft), about 4.5hr.

Not the West Highland Way: A Mountain High Way

Foul-weather alternative: Loch Sloy

Arrochar & Tarbet Station to Inverarnan by Loch Sloy
Distance   20.5km (13 miles)
Ascent   450m (1400ft)
Appoximate time   6hr

Arrochar & Tarbet Station to Inveruglas pier
Distance   10km (6 miles)
Ascent   150m (500ft)
Approximate time   3hr

For any high-level crossing, it's sensible to have a valley route in case of nasty weather. The one here is pleasant, if unexciting, along Glen Loin, then rather harsh beside Loch Sloy. A better way, if you can make the ferries work for you, would be to duck out before Loch Sloy to Inveruglas, and cross Loch Lomond to the regular West Highland Way at Inversnaid. Better still, if the weather forecast is clearly too uncomfortable for Ben Ime, would be to adjust your plans eastwards from the very start, and begin your walk off the bus at Balmaha.

Even though this low-level route is less pleasant than the regular WH Way on the other bonnie bank of Loch Lomond, it does have a rugged remoteness of its own, composed of spruce plantations, pylons, and an ugly reservoir.

Walkers at Coiregrogain below Ben Vane

ROUTE 18 – WRONG SIDE OF THE LOCH: THE ARROCHAR ALPS

From **Arrochar & Tarbet Station** pass under the railway and turn left on a path through woods around the base of Cruach Tairbeirt. After 1.5km keep ahead, signed 'Inveruglas', as a side-path on the left drops to Arrochar village.
The main path runs through woods to another signed junction, where you keep ahead for Inveruglas. The path runs up **Glen Loin**, parallel with two sets of pylons. It joins a track, which soon reverts back to being a wide, well-built footpath. It crosses a col with a small crag above, then another col under a pylon, and descends northwards in a wide, boggy tree gap.

Soon the path runs alongside trees on the left, then enters them for 500 metres. It bends right, across a field, to a kissing gate where it joins a track near **Coiregrogain**. Turn right, over Inveruglas Water, to join a tarred access track at a waymark post. For Inveruglas pier follow this tarmac track out to the right to the A82 at Loch Lomond, and turn left on a path alongside the road.

Turn left up this private road all the way to the base of **Loch Sloy** dam. Head up to the right-hand (eastern) end of the dam.

Ahead stretches **Loch Sloy**, described in a guidebook of 1949: 'surely no more beautiful hill loch exists in Scotland'. But now Loch Sloy lies sullen behind the concrete, between two lines of pylons, rimmed with reservoir-side rubble (unless the water level is really high). 'Loch Sloy' was the war-cry of the Macfarlanes, deadly folk hereabouts. Now there are no folk hereabouts.

From the dam end a small path teeters along the steep slope above the reservoir. As the slope relents, the ground becomes easier but the path itself harder to follow. Three quarters of the way up the loch, where it narrows, start heading slightly up the slope on the right, to round the corner of Ben Vorlich.

Stay just above the soggy valley floor for 1km, to meet a stream descending towards the main river (NN 284 146). This is the outflow from an artificial waterway or leat. There is a small track beyond the descending stream. Turn right, up this, in 500 metres joining a larger track.

Here there's a choice of ways. Easier, but less interesting, is to turn left across the valley floor for the track through the plantations on the left side of the valley. This track is the main route, described above. At the end of the track you'll have to cross the **Dubh-uisge**, which will be difficult or impossible after heavy rain.

Rather than turning down left across the valley, the slower but prettier alternative is to follow the track ahead along another leat. At its end, keep ahead along the leat, which is now covered, with a small path alongside. After just over 1km it ends (NN 299 156). Slant downhill, to join the power line at the valley floor just as the valley steepens. A rough quad-bike path is under the power lines. Follow it to the final pylon, where the valley and the power lines dip steeply out of sight.

Continue down through the wood to the A82 as on the main route.

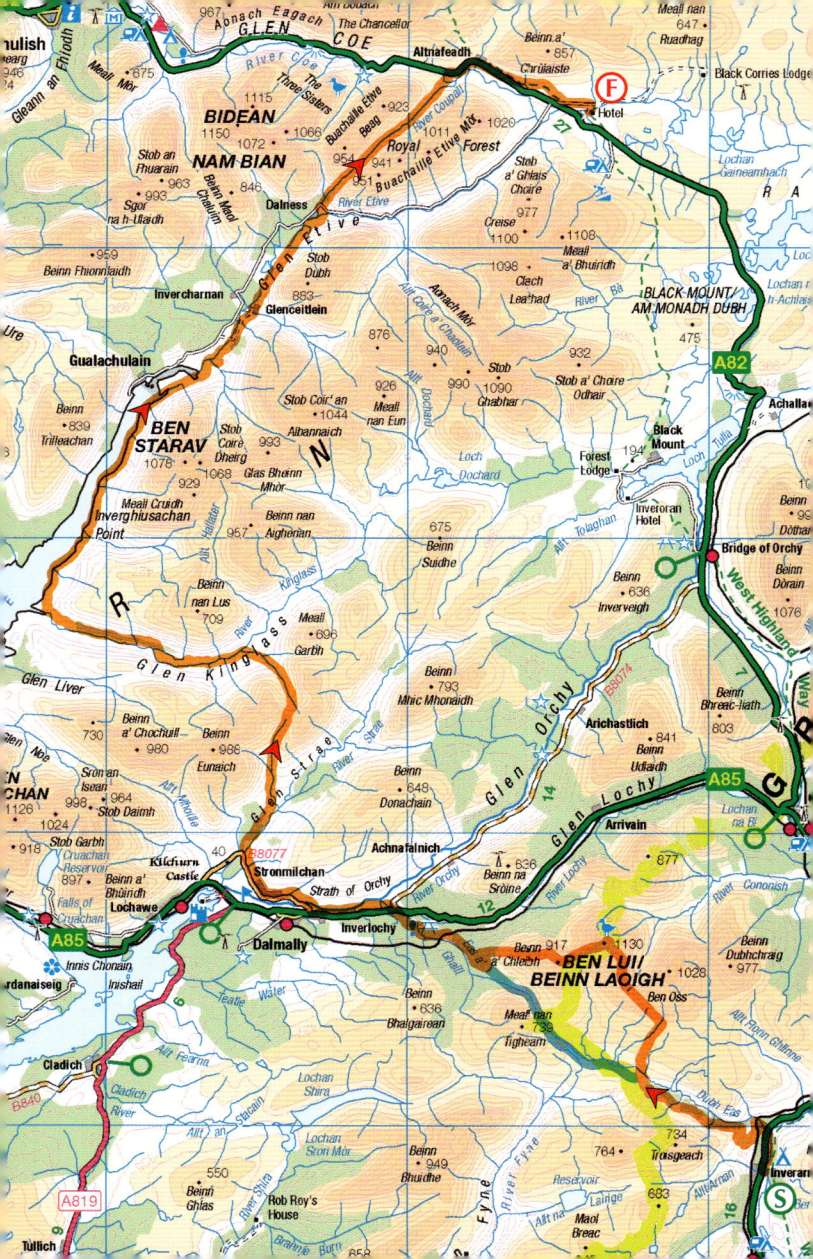

ROUTE 19

The Etive Trek

Start	Inverarnan
Finish	Kings House (or Kinlochleven)
Distance	79km (49 miles)
Ascent	2800m (9500ft)
Approximate time	24hr (3 full days)
Day 1	A high crossing of Ben Lui to Dalmally (bus, train, shops, accommodation)
Days 2–3	Low-level and gentler, but remote along Loch Etive to Kings House (bus, hotel)
(To Kinlochleven add 6km (4 miles), 300m (1000ft), about 2hr)	
Facilities	
Inverarnan (start)	Citylink coaches; nearest station Ardlui (ferry to Ardleish then 3km of WH Way); Drover's Inn, Beinglas campsite with café and shop
Dalmally	At Glenview, small shop (Glenview Stores) and Citylink coaches. At Dalmally, B&Bs, Glenorchy Lodge Hotel, station. Orchy Bank Guest House is on the B8077 just over Dalmally Bridge
Altnafeadh (end)	Citylink coaches
Kings House, Kinlochleven	See Appendix B

> What I think best is a stance inland from the salt water, where the mountain air, brushing over gall and heather, takes the sting from the sea air, and the two blended give a notion of the fine variousness of life.
> *Colin of Elrigmore, in John Splendid Neil Munro (1898)*

A route that crosses mountains every day eventually becomes exhausting. One that stays in the valleys misses out on the views. The answer is to alternate. While this branch route takes off over Ben Lui, the most majestic of the Southern Highlands, its second day is at sea level, all along the shore of Loch Etive.

The third day ought to be the decider – but in fact it stays neither high nor low. Instead it crosses two moderate passes, the Lairig Gartain followed by the Devil's Staircase on the West Highland Way.

Not the West Highland Way: A Mountain High Way

This is a rather remote and serious bit of backpacking. To start, although a surfaced track gets you in across the harsh lower ground, Ben Lui is crossed away from the popular paths. Beinn a' Chleibh is an outlying summit, awkward for Munro-baggers, but here crossed in natural style westwards on the way down to Dalmally. Here is a small shop, hotel and B&Bs.

Another barely visible path leads over the Lairig Dhoireann – once an important crossing northwards, now used only by the occasional shepherd. The path alongside Loch Etive is used by just enough folk each year to keep it visible on the ground.

For the final stage, we come back among the hill-baggers. The Lairig Gartain is an access path for Munros on either side, and the Devil's Staircase is, by comparison with what's led up to it, a busy street and almost urban. Its firm dry surface will be deservedly enjoyed as the easy way through to Kinlochleven. And Kinlochleven itself is the rest and resupply route for any number of fine routes on into the UK's biggest hills.

Track up Glen Kinglass, below Beinn Ceitlein

DAY 1
Inverarnan to Dalmally by Ben Lui

Start	Inverarnan
Finish	Dalmally (bridge)
Distance	27km (17 miles)
Ascent	1350m (4500ft)
Approximate time	9.5hr
Maximum altitude	Ben Lui 1130m
Terrain	Track and hill paths, then a rough grassy descent and forest gap, with tracks to finish

Ben Lui is the finest mountain of the Southern Highlands, and this is a splendidly straight southeast to northwest crossing of it. As a bonus, the natural line crosses what is otherwise an outlying nuisance Munro, Beinn a' Chleibh. The walk out to Dalmally includes some pleasant woodland.

The route up to Ben Lui is described fully in Route 6 (page 61). Briefly: from **Inverarnan,** a path alongside the road leads north to the road end of Beinglas campsite. Continue along the road for 1km to a tarmac track opposite Glen Falloch Farm. The track crosses the railway, and climbs uphill, with views of Loch Lomond. Under power lines, turn right. The track runs high above **Gleann nan Caorann** for 4km, then divides. Turn down right, joining a huge pipeline across the valley floor and up to just below its top. Decision time: the bad-weather alternative turns away here.

Just below the top end of the pipe, turn right onto a track that crosses a stream bridge then climbs on, to the 550m contour. Slant up left, northwest, rising into the Lui/Oss col. Head up the grassy ridge north, then northwest as the broad ridge becomes more defined and a path forms, to the airy summit of **Ben Lui**. Inverarnan to Ben Lui 13.5km (8½ miles), 1200m (4000ft), about 5.5hr.

The path leads down around the corrie rim, with a small rocky moment avoidable down to the left. Just at the start of the short ridge leading towards the northwest top, a stony path turns down left for Beinn a' Chleibh.

The rough but clear path runs down Ben Lui's southwest spur, not unreasonably steep. The right edge of the spur is defined by intermittent crags, but the path keeps about 50 metres to left of what would otherwise be a useful navigational handrail. Cross the well-defined ridge across the 776m col, and up to the 916m summit of **Beinn a' Chleibh**. Here the path ends.

NOT THE WEST HIGHLAND WAY: A MOUNTAIN HIGH WAY

Southeast ridge of Ben Lui, looking across to the Crianlarich hills An Caisteal and Beinn Chabhair

Descend very gently northwest for 600 metres to a cairn, then as the ground steepens turn west down a grassy ridge. Follow it right down to a deer fence at the top of trees (NN 227 260). If you head down into a corner of the fence, you'll find a small hole to creep through. Below the fence, the ridgeline is tree-free, so just follow it down to reach a wide, smooth forest road.

Turn left for 500 metres, to meet a clearing under some power lines. Turn down a rough quad-bike track under the power lines as they dip towards Allt Coire Lair. Just before this stream, at a small weather station, an old track turns off right, into the trees. Follow this down through attractive woodland, past **Succoth Lodge** and under the railway, to turn right on a wider track and reach the A85. Turn left for 3km to pass **Glenview**. In another 400 metres, just before **Dalmally**, turn off right on the B8077 towards Stronmilchan. Ben Lui to Dalmally (bridge) 13km (8 miles), 150m (500ft), about 4hr.

ROUTE 19 – THE ETIVE TREK

Inverarnan to Dalmally: lower-level alternative

Distance	22.5km (14 miles)
Ascent	550m (1800ft)
Approximate time	7hr

This natural through-route, a crow-flight straight line to Dalmally, is mostly on enjoyable rough tracks across the moors. But the central 5km across the pass is on a damp quad-bike path over peaty grassland. We and the metaphorical crow are not the first to exploit this gap in the hills. The high-voltage power cables, overhead the entire way, slightly spoil the lovely view of Ben Cruachan.

Follow the main route up **Gleann nan Caorann**, and across the valley beside the large water pipe.

Follow the track right up the pipeline, and bend left around the pipeline's top to join a stony track. It passes under the power lines and heads up the broad valley of **Allt nan Caorainn**. Some track stones show reddish-brown excrescences, which are garnets. After 2km the track runs along the riverbank to end at a ford.

Don't cross the ford, but keep ahead on a path formed by quad bikes. It runs through damp peaty grassland northwest, gradually rising to join the power pylons as they cross the south ridge of Beinn a' Chleibh. The wheelmark path runs under the power lines, grassy and fairly firm.

After three pylons the path and power lines turn downhill towards Strath Orchy, with grand views of Cruachan. They keep to right of the stream, to a gate in a deer fence. The plantations beyond are broken by a wide clearing under the power lines. This new stream is Allt a' Chaorainn, the Stream of Rowan Trees. The earlier one was Allt nan Caorainn, the Stream of The Rowan Trees. It is not uncommon for streams on either side of a pass to share a Gaelic name. It'll happen again tomorrow.

The wheelmarks track continues, sometimes wet, down the clearing. After 1km the track edges left into the trees, but regains the clearing to cross a wide, smooth forest road. The rough track continues down the clearing beyond.

Just before Allt Coire Lair there's a small weather station, and a track crosses the clearing. Turn right down this, into trees, then through clear-felled ground. The disused track runs pleasantly through alder, hazel and oak above Eas a' Ghaill, to **Succoth Lodge**.

Pass between the buildings onto a stony track. It passes under the railway through a narrow arch, then reaches a wide, smooth forest road. Turn right, downhill, for 3km to reach the A85. Turn left for 3km to **Glenview**, with **Dalmally** just ahead.

Not the West Highland Way: A Mountain High Way

DAY 2
Dalmally to Loch Etive Head

Start	Dalmally (bridge)
Finish	Loch Etive Head
Distance	30km (19 miles)
Ascent	900m (2000ft)
Approximate time	9.5hr
Maximum altitude	Lairig Dhoireann 615m
Terrain	Paths, sometimes faint in places and soft, and 5km of good track

From the junction just east of Dalmally, follow the B8077 over **River Orchy**, past a distinctive octagonal church, and through Stronmilchan. After 3km cross a bridge over River Strae: at once, and before a second bridge, a track turns off right (with a parking area at its beginning).

In 500 metres take the left fork, past a building and then a long pool on the right, to another track junction. Keep ahead on the main track, which has returned from Duiletter bridge. At the end of plantations, there's a pool on the right with a pine island. In another 1km, the track approaches a bridge over **Allt Dhoirrean**.

Before this bridge, turn left uphill through a field gate, on faint quad-bike tracks. (A path to right of the stream looks tempting but turns unhelpfully aside higher up the hill.) The track is faint, but if you lose it the going is rough grassland, comfortable enough.

The faint quad track, along with an even fainter old stalkers' path, heads up to left of the stream. Finally a few cairns mark the old path line into the **Lairig Dhoireann** col. Go straight through; traces of path continue down alongside Allt Dhoireann (different stream, same name) to the valley floor. If you plan to continue to Inveroran and Bridge of Orchy by Route 16: cross beside Allt Dhoireann's collapsing footbridge for faint riverside paths leading 1km upstream to a dangly bridge over River Kinglass.

Turn left, using traces of path and wheelmarks of quad bikes to follow **River Kinglass** downstream. After 1.2km you reach a substantial new bridge for Landrovers, leading over to the well-built track on the north side of the river. Dalmally to River Kinglass 13.5km (8½ miles), 600m (1900ft), about 5hr.

As you cross the river, you can at once turn left into an older track close to the river; and this will give pleasanter walking than the smooth harsh new one at various points down the valley.

ROUTE 19 – THE ETIVE TREK

Down Glen Etive to Loch Etive, from Buachaille Etive Beag

At the valley end, as the track bends left towards its bridge over the River Kinglass, take a track on the right to pass **Ardmaddy**. A smaller track leads past the house to Loch Etive and a ruined pier. The track becomes a path along the high-tide mark, keeping left of a fenced enclosure. This path is hard to find at first, then gets clearer. Mostly it is small but good, with a few boggy bits.

After 3km you'll cross Allt Ghiusachan – which may be awkward after heavy rain, judging by the wide swathe of spate-carried boulders. The small path continues along the loch shore, in places very wet. At least one more river crossing would give problems in spate conditions. The path hauls past Beinn Trilleachan with its granite slabs on the other side of the sea loch, to reach Loch Etive's head. Here the path keeps along the foot of the steep slope on the right.

The hut at Kinlochetive was a bothy at one time but no longer, now taken over by Venture Scouts for disadvantaged young people. It's a convenient breakpoint for the section, but tempting camp sites are all along Loch Etive. Kinglass footbridge to Kinlochetive 16.5km (10½ miles), about 4 hr.

NOT THE WEST HIGHLAND WAY: A MOUNTAIN HIGH WAY

DAY 3
Loch Etive Head to Kings House

Start	Loch Etive Head (Kinlochetive)
Finish	Kings House (or Kinlochleven)
Distance	21.5km (13½ miles)
Ascent	550m (1800ft)
Approximate time	6hr
Maximum altitude	Lairig Gartain 485m
Terrain	Paths, mostly good, but small in Glen Etive

After Kinlochetive hut a wider path continues along the foot of the right-hand slope. It joins **River Etive**, but soon turns up right along a sidestream. After a double footbridge, you turn back down the sidestream (Allt Mheuran) to rejoin River Etive. After **Coleitir** the path becomes a track which soon turns down left towards River Etive. Here fork right on a smaller track to Glenceitlein.

At the house bear right on a rough track. It becomes a small, old path which passes above a steep curve of the river opposite Lochan Urr, then it descends to the riverside flood plain. The path follows the foot of the hill slope, then the riverbank. Above Dalness house, cross a stout bridge, turn briefly downstream, then head right to the road bridge over Allt Lairig Eilde. A few steps down-valley,

Lairig Gartain and Buachaille Etive Beag

Dalness, River Etive and Lairig Gartain below Buachaille Etive Mor

a green SRWS (now 'ScotWays') signpost points uphill. The path heads up in trees, forking right over a stream then straight up the spur that is the southwest end of Buachaille Etive Beag. It passes through a protective deer fence into a replanted wood, carries on directly uphill, and at 250m altitude emerges again through an upper deer fence.

Just above this, turn right on a path that contours around the hill nose, then gradually rises to join the **Allt Gartain** stream. The path continues rather steeply uphill, to left of the stream, to reach the **Lairig Gartain** pass.

The path is marked by cairns through the pass, and continues gently downhill to left of the new stream which is the beginning of River Coupall. The path is peaty and in places soft. Emerging from the valley foot, it keeps ahead (northeast) across boggy ground to a car park on the A82.

Cross, to find a remnant of old road leading to the right. It soon rejoins the A82, which must be followed for the last 500 metres to **Altnafeadh**. Kinlochetive to Altnafeadh 17km (10½ miles), 500m (1700ft), about 5hr.

Here is a bus stop for Glasgow and Fort William, and also a corner of the West Highland Way. For Kings House, and the crossing of Rannoch Moor, you'd follow the WH Way for 4.5km to the right, eastwards. But for a well-earned hot shower and soft bed follow the West Highland Way ahead over the Devil's Staircase to Kinlochleven. See 'Kings House to Kinlochleven' in Part 1 for route details. Altnafeadh to Kinlochleven 9.5km (6 miles), 300m (1000ft), about 3hr.

ROUTE 20
Blackwater and the Lairig Leacach

Start	Kinlochleven
Finish	Spean Bridge (or Fort William)
Distance	40km (25 miles)
Ascent	700m (2400ft)
Approximate time	12hr (a long day and a short one)
Maximum altitude	Lairig Leacach 460m
Terrain	Small paths, sometimes wet or rough

(Route 11 offers a short-cut in from Kings House to the Blackwater Dam.)

Kinlochleven to Corrour Station
Distance	23.5km (14½ miles)
Ascent	600m (2000ft)
Approximate time	7hr

Kinlochleven to Fort William via Loch Treig
Distance	47km (29 miles)
Ascent	500m (1700ft)
Approximate time	13hr (two short days)

Facilities
Kinlochleven (start)	Buses to Ballachulish (for Citylink coaches) and Fort William
Loch Chiarain	Bothy
Staoineag, Meanach (on Glen Nevis alternative)	Bothies
Corrour Station	Restaurant, B&B; youth hostel Loch Ossian (year-round)
Lairig Leacach	Bothy
Spean Bridge	Shop, hotels; trains and Citylink coach

Route 15 was what I consider the best beginner's backpack: two short days from Kinlochleven to Fort William by Glen Nevis. This is a wilder version, with boggier paths, a remoter bothy, and a high pass through the Lairig Leacach to Spean Bridge. Here are the woodland and waterfalls of the River Leven, and a wild lochan in the heart of the hills. At the Treig reservoir, the bleak loneliness is only emphasised by the clatter of the train, three times a day, as it works its way along the far side of the water. The folk inside, with their earbuds and plastic

ROUTE 20 – BLACKWATER AND THE LAIRIG LEACACH

snacks, are patiently reading their hillwalking magazines while waiting for the coffee trolley. They may be only a mile away, but they're in a different world.

At Loch Treig you could turn left and take Glen Nevis through to Fort William, as in Route 15. But ahead, Lairig Leacach is a proper hill pass. You're high, but the rugged mountains on either side rise a whole lot higher. Deer stroll across the slopes, white water tumbles down from either side, and as those sides close in there's another bothy, just exactly where you wanted it. Then a handy track leads down and out to Spean Bridge.

This particular trek comes recommended by one of Scotland's outstanding experts in long-distance hiking: James Grahame, the Marquis of Montrose (see box below).

This is the trek with everything – at least insofar as 'everything' can be contained within two shortish days on the trail and 350 years of history. And it's also, if you choose to cross the Great Glen and keep going, the gateway to the even wilder wilderness. Paths head onwards for days, or weeks, all the way to the blanket bogs of Sutherland and Cape Wrath.

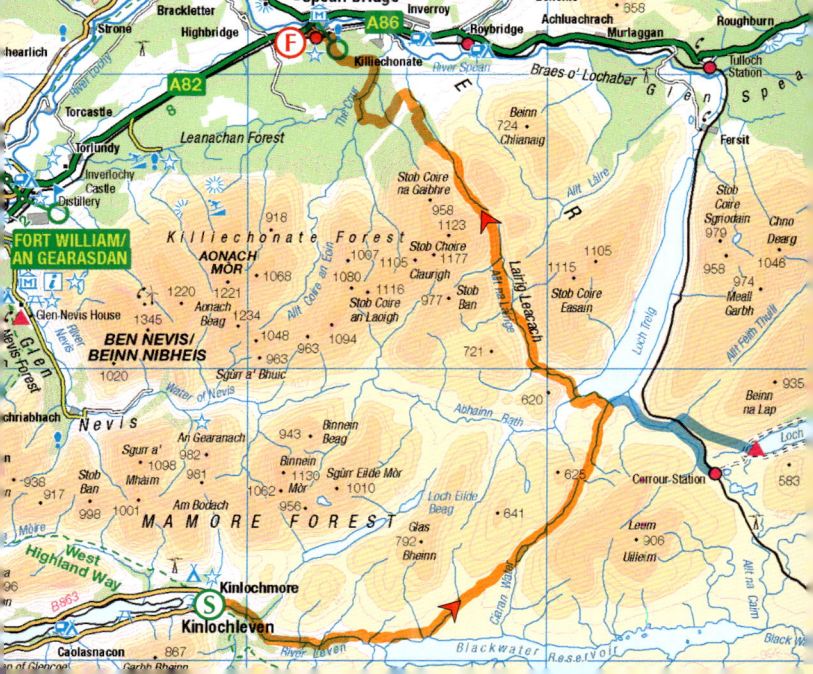

Not the West Highland Way: A Mountain High Way

> ## MONTROSE'S MARCH 1645
>
> In 1645 the Marquis of Montrose was in command of an army of 1500 men (mostly MacDonalds) on behalf of King Charles II against Oliver Cromwell, but actually battling traditional clan enemies the Campbells. After sacking Inveraray, Montrose and his men headed up into the Great Glen. The Marquess of Argyll, with 3000 Campbells, followed up Glen Etive (Route 19) and the WH Way behind him. Montrose, at Fort Augustus, found himself trapped between this Campbell army at Inverlochy (Fort William), and another anti-royalist army at Inverness. It was 31 January, and the hills on either side were deep in snow.
>
> His solution was one of the boldest acts of military backpacking in British history. His first day took his 1500 men up the Corrieyairack pass and down Glen Roy to Roybridge in Glen Spean. The exact route isn't known, but can't have been less than 35km with 600m of ascent (22 miles and 2000ft). That's about 10 hours' walking as times have been reckoned in this book, but Montrose and his MacDonalds had only eight hours of daylight, through snowdrifts, carrying all their provisions, broadswords, shields, and the man-high Lochaber axe.
>
> The second day's march is also uncertain. It may have been along the northern flank of the Nevis Range. However, some historians have them following parts of the present route. After a cold night without campfires they forded the icy River Spean, then would have come up through the Lairig Leacach to Luibeilt, and down the full length of Glen Nevis. That's 30km (18½ miles) and 550m (1800ft) – a mere 8.5 hours as reckoned in this book. At dawn on the third day, they emerged from Glen Nevis, surprised Argyll's army that outnumbered them two to one, and defeated it. Clach nan Caimbeulach, the Cairn, is at the northern entrance to the Lairig Mor. It marks where the exhausted MacDonalds gave up their pursuit of the battered Campbells back down the West Highland Way.

From **Kinlochleven**'s main bridge over River Leven a tarred path starts at a WH Way marker board and runs upstream through woodland near the river. It passes opposite the tailrace from the hydroelectric works. Just before emerging onto Wade Road, turn right on a path under fir trees near the river. Emerge to the end of Wade Road, and turn right on its continuation track to a junction. Just to the right is a bridge used by the WH Way, but keep ahead on a small path marked as **Ciaran Path**.

Route 20 – Blackwater and the Lairig Leach

Loch Treig, from the track to Corrour

Keep ahead on this path, which runs through woods above and to left of **River Leven**. After the footbridge over the sidestream Allt na h-Eilde, the path climbs with a view to waterfalls on the left. Soon there's another striking waterfall to see across the valley (or there is if spare water is being released at the top of the hydro pipe).

The path descends gently to a riverside meadow, passing concrete pillars that were the bases of huts housing prisoners from World War II. The path continues in woods above the river, with a variety of grey schist and pinkish rhyolite underfoot, and small waterfalls above. It dips into a little gorge, with a ruined bridge, but an easy crossing anyway. Then it climbs rather eroded onto moorland, passing above two lochans to join the high pipeline from Loch Eilde.

Keep ahead to pass the **Blackwater dam**'s end. Sketchy paths continue just above the shore of Blackwater Reservoir. A better path soon forms about 200 metres up from the reservoir, a forgotten stalkers' path. It bends left alongside the small river Allt an Inbhir, with a Celtic cross monument on the opposite side. As the river turns north, the path crosses it and keeps its previous direction (northeast) over a spur. It drops to join a new stream, follows it briefly, then contours to

FOR CORROUR STATION, LOCH OSSIAN OR FORT WILLIAM

Loch Ossian Youth Hostel, evening, with Ben Nevis

On reaching the track at Loch Treig turn right. After 800 metres the track climbs away from the loch to a bridge under the railway. (For Loch Ossian, go under the railway: see following paragraph.) Staying to right of the railway, cross a rough stream bridge and bear right to join the remains of an old track. This runs uphill to right of the railway. It crosses Allt a' Chamabhreac twice, then levels towards Corrour Station. The last 400 metres is swampy. To save your socks and the Scotrail carpets, bear left off the track line to a small path alongside the railway. Follow it to the level crossing alongside Corrour Station.

For Loch Ossian Stay on the main track as it runs under the railway alongside a stream, then crosses that stream. It runs southeast around the base of Beinn na Lap (sometimes nominated as Scotland's dullest Munro). After 2km short-cut right down a rough old track. As it dives into a small swamp there's a footbridge on the right. The track joins a smooth firm one near the head of Loch Ossian. Here turn right, and at the next junction turn left for the youth hostel (and, eventually, Dalwhinnie – see Route 22). Loch Chiarain to Corrour 11.5km (7 miles), 200m (700ft), about 3hr. Loch Chiarain 12km (7½ miles), 400m (1300ft), about 4 hours.

For Glen Nevis and Fort William On reaching the bridge over Abhainn Rath you'll need to turn left, upstream. There are paths on both sides of the river. If you want Staoineag bothy, head upstream to left of the river. Otherwise

ROUTE 20 – BLACKWATER AND THE LAIRIG LEACACH

you'll find better paths if you cross the slippery wooden bridge and head upstream to the river's right.

There are white waterslides, with alder trees hanging over, and grassy meadows to camp on, as well as soggy tussocky ones that are less tempting for the tent. After 2km you pass opposite Staoineag bothy. In another 3km you reach the bothy at Meanach. The continuation to Glen Nevis and Fort William is in Route 15 (Part 2). Loch Treig to Meanach 5.5km (3½ miles), about 1.5hr.

---

the bothy at the foot of **Loch Chiarain**. Kinlochleven to Loch Chiarain 12km (7½ miles), 400m (1300ft), about 4 hours.

The main path runs above the bothy, and along the left shore of the small loch. The way is obvious, through the hill slot directly ahead. This is just as well, as the small path itself can be lost. Keep to the left-hand side of the pass, along the foot of the steep ground. There are remains of old enclosures through the pass.

The pass descends as **Gleann Iolairean**, whose name promises eagles overhead. The path runs just above the valley floor on the steep left-hand slope. As the valley opens out the path slants left, away from the stream, to join a track alongside **Loch Treig**.

For Corrour Station turn right here (see previous page); otherwise follow the track to the left around the loch head, to reach a slippery and unparapeted bridge over Abhainn Rath. (Here you could turn left for Glen Nevis: again see box opposite.) Loch Chiarain to Loch Treig 7.5km (4½ miles), about 2hr.

However, the main way ahead is for Spean Bridge by Lairig Leacach. So cross the slippery bridge over Abhainn Rath, and continue around the reservoir past the boarded-up lodge at **Creaguaineach**. The reservoir shore becomes a riverbank leading up to the left. A path rises to a gate into a small fenced enclosure. At once, a path down to the right leads to a footbridge under the first trees.

This path, to right (east) of **Allt na Lairige** river, has better views of its waterfalls but is very small. (For the path to left or west of the river don't drop to the footbridge, but climb slightly through the col behind a small knoll and then drop right, to the riverbank, above waterfalls. This path is alongside the river and mostly clear.)

As the valley opens out, the path on the east side disappears, so you'll probably cross the river and join the clearer one on the west side. There's a new footbridge (NN 2858 7195) built for quad bikes. After this the path is soggy and overlain by quad-bike tracks in parts. It reaches another new footbridge over Allt a' Chuil Choirean. **Lairig Leacach bothy** is just beyond. Loch Treig to Lairig Leacach 6km (4 miles), 250m (750ft), about 2.5hr.

Creaguaineach Lodge on Loch Treig

ROUTE 20 – BLACKWATER AND THE LAIRIG LEACACH

High camp at Lochan Rath, above Lairig Leacach

From the bothy, head on up the good track through the beautiful hill pass. It descends to left of the new stream, then crosses it, and runs down through a felled plantation. The track then runs down through an open field (or walk in the field alongside the river) to a signpost on the left for Spean Bridge. If short of time or tired, head on down the track to Corriechoille, and follow the tarmac lane along the River Spean quite pleasantly to Spean Bridge.

The signed track runs into a gloomy plantation but will have proper woodland later. After 2km turn down right on a smaller, grassier track again signed for Spean Bridge. After 700 metres, as the track bends right, take the path down left signed for Spean Bridge. It leads across a footbridge under birches.

At the junction beyond turn right, on a cycle path above the river. Another footbridge crosses Allt a' Chois, and another bike path joins from the left. Soon (at NN 242 803) the path becomes an old track.

Ignore a side-track on the right (down to Killiechonate). The old track ahead climbs slightly, after 1km becomes cycle path, and in another 200 metres bends right at a forest ride. Continue over a rise and down to cross a track. The path descends until it bends right, at which point turn left on the track immediately below. After 200 metres, as the track contours forward, take a path forking down right with a waymark post 'station'. It runs through woods to emerge just above **Spean Bridge Station**. Lairig Leacach bothy to Spean Bridge 14.5km (9 miles), 3.5hr.

Not the West Highland Way: A Mountain High Way

ROUTE 21
Routes of Rannoch

Start	Kings House
Finish	Corrour Station
Distance	36.5km (23 miles)
Ascent	1050m (3200ft)
Approximate time	12hr (two short days)
Facilities	
Kings House (start)	Citylink coaches, hotel
Rannoch Station	Café, shop, museum (closed winter); Moor of Rannoch Hotel
Corrour Station (end)	Restaurant, B&B; youth hostel Loch Ossian (year-round); trains (on the current timetable the 6.25pm train south connects at Bridge of Orchy with a Citylink coach to Kings House)

The Black Mount, Buachaille Etive Mor, Ben Alder; mighty mountains all. But more unnerving than any of them is the flat granite ground lying in between. Rannoch Moor, 14 miles of heather and black bog and a hundred shining lochans. Still, black rivers 20 metres wide wind unpredictably among the black hags. On crisp autumn days the sun shines on the mountaintops, but cold mist lies all day across the Moor of Rannoch and the heather is pale with hoar frost. Here, in the Ice Age, was the highest, thickest point at the centre of Scotland's icecap. The ice carried Rannoch's granite boulders outwards, using them as sandpaper to grind the radial glens to south, west and east.

Glencoe MacDonalds raided this way, into Lochaber and southwards to Breadalbane and the Lowlands. Returning with the stolen cows, they only had to step into the wide heather and the peat hags, and pursuit became a waste of time. Cattle drovers made their hill road around the edge, along the safer slope of the Black Mount, and so did the soldiers of Major Caulfeild – the aim was to pacify the Highlands people, not the black peat of Rannoch.

Today, the Landrover track might be thought to tame it. But actually, it's an advantage. It takes you far enough in so that you can't contemplate turning all the way back out again. It takes you in, and then it dumps you off, in the middle of the 14 miles of granite hummocks, and peat banks, and slow

ROUTE 21 – ROUTES OF RANNOCH

> winding rivers of black water. For eight miles ahead is the heather, and the tussock grass, and a black path where the boot sinks to the ankle.
> For Rannoch Moor is, quite simply, Scotland's biggest bog.

In front of us there lay a piece of low, broken, desert land, which we must now cross. The sun was not long up, and shone straight in our eyes; a little, thin mist went up from the face of the moorland like a smoke…
The mist rose and died away, and showed us that country lying as waste as the sea; only the moor fowl and the peewees crying upon it, and far over to the east a herd of deer, moving like dots. Much of it was red with heather; much of the rest broken up with bogs and hags and peaty pools; some had been burnt black with fire; and in another place there was quite a forest of dead firs, standing like skeletons.
Kidnapped Robert Louis Stevenson (1886)

Now I saw in my Dream, that just as they had ended this talk, they drew near to a very miry Slough, that was in the midst of the plain; and they, being heedless, did both fall suddenly into the bog. The name of the slough was Dispond. Here therefore they wallowed for a time, being grievously bedaubed with the dirt; and Christian, because of the Burden that was on his back, began to sink in the mire.
Pilgrim's Progress John Bunyan (1678)

Rannoch Moor from Meall Mor

NOT THE WEST HIGHLAND WAY: A MOUNTAIN HIGH WAY

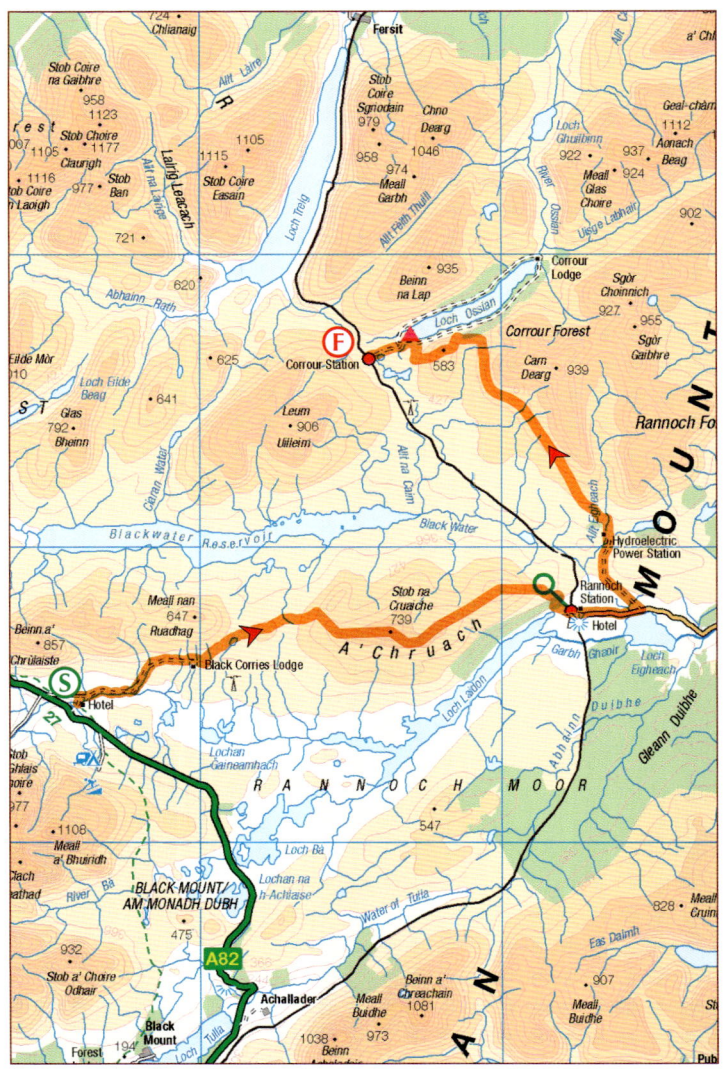

DAY 1

Kings House to Rannoch Station by A' Chruach

Distance	19km (12 miles)
Ascent	650m (2200ft)
Approximate time	7hr
Maximum altitude	Stob na Cruaiche 739m
Terrain	Track and rough path, then rough peaty grassland

From **Kings House** cross the bridge of the old road. At the next bend, turn right through a gate on the track towards Black Corries Lodge. The infant River Etive runs on your right. After 4km from Kings House, the track is about to enter the trees around **Black Corries Lodge**; immediately before this, turn left up a firm but rough path, with an SRWS signpost. It passes above the plantation with the lodge, and rejoins the track just beyond. This track, extended in the 2010s, offers an easier but less interesting route to Rannoch Station. Followed ahead, it becomes a peaty path, to the start of a new track through plantations on the north side of Loch Laidon.

The track is now much rougher. In 200 metres it forks. Take the rough stony track up left, northeast.

This leads to a rough bridge of sleepers immediately west of **Lochan Meall a' Phuill**. This track and its continuation quad-bike path follow the line of the stalkers' path marked on Landranger maps. A rough quad-bike path continues

Rannoch Moor from Rannoch Station

Descending to Rannoch Station

ROUTE 21 – ROUTES OF RANNOCH

northeast through the peat, reinforced with scrap timber and corrugated iron at the really soggy bits. It passes the head of the lochan and up onto Meall a' Phuill. Then it crosses the wide col beyond, and climbs east.

As the slope eases at the 500m contour, bear off right. Head straight uphill onto Stob nan Losgann. Keep east, on shortish grass. The going is pleasant, the views are great. (For the real Rannoch, perhaps you should be struggling through the tussocks on the other side of Loch Laidon). Occasional small cairns mark the regional boundary (Highland/Perthshire). Ascend gently east to the summit of **Stob na Cruaiche**. Kings House to Stob na Cruaiche 11.5km (7 miles), 600m (2000ft), about 4hr.

At the concrete pillar trig, bear half-right. Descend southeast at first, then follow a line of low humps above Loch Laidon, thus staying to right of the peat hags that lie on the Highland side of the boundary line. Bend northeast over Point 638, with its two memorial cairns. Keep northeast through a wide flat col, keeping to right of peat hags, and ascend rough heathery grass to the final lump of the ridge, **Meall Liath na Doire**.

Descend east, aiming just left of distant, pointed Schiehallion. At 430m is the top of a track, at a point where there was once a radio mast. Head down the track for 200 metres, then turn right down a side-track. This zigzags down open hill then through a short belt of trees, to a deer-fence gate. Climb over this locked gate and turn left on a track to the level crossing immediately to right of **Rannoch Station**.

Rannoch Station

NOT THE WEST HIGHLAND WAY: A MOUNTAIN HIGH WAY

DAY 2
Rannoch Station to Corrour by Road to the Isles

Distance	17.5km (11 miles)
Ascent	300m (1000ft)
Approximate time	5hr
Maximum altitude	Before Corrour Old Lodge 560m
Terrain	Minor road, track and good path

Follow the narrow road ahead past a 'Welcome to Perth & Kinross' sign (your right foot has actually been in P&K since A' Chruach). At once the road passes the Moor

Corrour Station with Leum Uilleim above

ROUTE 21 – ROUTES OF RANNOCH

of Rannoch Hotel. In 2km cross a bridge alongside **Loch Eigheach**, and in another 400 metres turn sharp left up a track with an SRWS signpost.

The track ascends gently northwest, then contours north around the hill flank to join **Allt Eigheach** (a small river). Cross a rough bridge to left of the track, and head up the bank to left of the river. The main track soon fords the river to rejoin you. Keep ahead on the track to pass to right of a pine plantation, and bend left at its corner.

The wide, smooth new track heads northwest, gradually working up the side of Sron Leachd a' Chaorainn. It levels, with wide views across the moor and along Blackwater Reservoir; then descends gently, passing below the ruins of **Corrour Old Lodge**.

The path bends round the hill flank, north. In 3km from the ruin, the hump Meall na Lice is down on your left. Here a wide stony path turns down left. Follow

Looking across Rannoch Moor to distant Ben Nevis

it gradually down to the head of **Loch Ossian**. If there's time, do divert over the rugged but rewarding Meall na Lice to reach the hill path across its west flank – an extra 0.5km with 100m of ascent, less than 30min. The path meets a track at the loch head, with the youth hostel directly ahead. Turn left along the track, following it south of west and gently uphill to **Corrour Station**.

PART FOUR
Roads to the Deep North

The track to Culra bothy

PART 4 – ROADS TO THE DEEP NORTH

Clouds move on the wind
I know I have to walk on
by the sea, northwards

Before setting out on the *Narrow Road to the Deep North* (1689), from which these lines are taken, the poet Basho sold his house and wrote his will. His 3000-mile route from Tokyo crossed many high summits and took 156 days.

Loch Lomond to Fort William is just the start. First you walk the high hilly places alongside the West Highland Way. Then you get a tent and take a two-day test trip out of Kinlochleven. Then you get a slightly better tent, strengthen your shoulders, and hike northwards in shop-hop stages right through the Southern Highlands. And next spring, something bigger and even better: the northwest Highlands, or the Cairngorms, or even Knoydart.

But maybe you can't wait that long. Maybe you've got to Fort William, and there's a handy supermarket to restock at, and those new blister plasters you bought just feel so good on the feet. For there's no way the Great Glen is the end. In Scotland the only real reason to stop is the sea.

Alongside Loch Hourn, northwest Highlands

ROUTE 22
Corrour to Dalwhinnie

Start	Corrour Station
Finish	Dalwhinnie
Distance	37km (23 miles)
Ascent	400m (1400ft)
Approximate time	10hr (two short days)
Maximum altitude	Bealach Dubh 725m (The Fara 911m)
Terrain	Tracks and paths
Facilities	
Corrour Station (start)	Trains; B&B, youth hostel Loch Ossian (year-round but often fully booked)
Culra	Bothy
Dalwhinnie	Trains and coaches, café, hotel and distillery

On the overview maps at the start of this book, Corrour appears at the top right-hand corner. It's not. For backpackers with big ambition, Corrour is the bit at the beginning. The next stage will be eastwards to Dalwhinnie, gateway to the eastern Grampians. For backpackers with a bit more restraint, Corrour to Dalwhinnie is the second half of a long long-weekend, with a sleeper train south at the end of it.

As a bonus, Dalwhinnie is one of three claimants to highest village in the Highlands (360m/1050ft – the other two are Braemar and Tomintoul). This, of course, means the trek ends with less downhill to damage your ankles.

Starting at the middle of nowhere brings the problem of how to arrive in the first place. There's the direct sleeper train from London Euston; the train pulls away and leaves you under the stars somewhere on Rannoch Moor, wondering at the black lumpy hills around the horizon and hoping you can lay hand on the headtorch. You could take the train to Rannoch, and walk the second day of Route 21. You could arrive from Kinlochleven by Route

20. Or, for a supremely satisfying straight line eastwards, walk from Fort William by romantic Glen Nevis, Route 20 (alternative) in reverse.

All these paths (plus one from Spean Bridge) converge onto one of Scotland's top nightspots, the eco-themed youth hostel sticking out into Loch Ossian. The stag stands at the back door hoping you'll throw your three-day sandwich out. What the stag didn't notice is that he's on one of the three sides of the hostel that's actually loch. Knee-deep in Loch Ossian, you might spot him on the Hostelling Scotland website.

A smooth track takes you to the head of **Loch Ossian**, where you pass a fantasy shooting lodge built in granite and glass. A stalkers' path leads on northeast, to left of Uisge Labhair, into the wide valley. Follow the stalkers' path until it peters out; then strike up right to find another one, leading up into the pass called **Bealach Dubh**.

Through the pass, the paths of Benalder Estate are well maintained, so you can re-enact the comfortable stride of the Victorian deer stalker but without the hairy tweed and the horrid hobnails. You could camp somewhere in this peaty place, and spend the rest of the day on Ben Alder. It's the remotest hill of the Southern Highlands, and also one of the biggest. As a reward, there's a ramshackle ridge of mossy schisty blocks, the **Long Leacas**, as a way down again. (It's the northeast corner of the hill and a barely Grade 1 scramble.) Otherwise, the path leads easily down to **Culra bothy**. Corrour Station to Culra 21km (13 miles), 350m (1200ft), about 6hr.

Just downstream is a dangly footbridge. The path beyond leads northeast, to join a smooth Landrover track down to **Loch Ericht**. The good development of Benalder includes a granite château at the side of the loch. With its towers and great entrance, it requires only a troupe of precocious child actors to double as Harry Potter's Hogwarts. However, the track out along the loch is harsh for peat-softened feet. So I prefer the high way, ignoring the track altogether to pass from Loch Pattack along the long ridge of **The Fara**. An almost-made-it Munro, The Fara is just 3m too low to have anybody else about.

It's possible to descend rather steeply southeast off The Fara through a tree gap, and get the granite château anyway in your walk. Culra to Dalwhinnie by Loch Ericht track 16km (10 miles), 50m (150ft), about 4hr; by The Fara 17km (10½ miles), 500m (1700ft), about 5.5hr.

Not the West Highland Way: A Mountain High Way

Onwards and eastwards

The eastern Grampians are where it gets less interesting. The A9 hills – the waggish sometimes spell them as Aighen Eidhean (pronounced Ay-en Iy-en) – are where the moorland heaves itself with a groan to just above the 3000ft Munro mark – then sinks with a splash back into the peat. Dalwhinnie has the essential facilities for what is the main access point to these eastern Grampians. It has a distillery, so you can get drunk; and a railway station, so you can get the heck out of here.

Your rucksack thuds damply into the corner of the sleeping car. You could dine in the dining car while night gathers among the drumlins of Drumochter. But perhaps you're discouraged by the way your dry dining-clothes are a skimpy T-shirt and a pair of orange long johns, and it would be even more delicious to finish off those well-travelled sandwiches in bed while watching the peat passing the windows. All this is most enjoyable, but even more so because you don't have to haul the soggy sack onwards across those peaty moors.

But just supposing you don't take that so-tempting train, you've a harsh day ahead. One way over the moors is the track at the end of Corrie Chuaich: this takes you up onto the moorland, and after 2km, a still-visible stalkers' path takes you down again to Gaick Lodge. Head up the Allt Bhran, where a track leads through to Ruigh-aiteachain in Glen Feshie.

Glen Feshie, gateway to the Cairngorms

ROUTE 23 – FORT WILLIAM TO INVERIE

Glen Feshie is altogether unlike Glen Nevis. Here are grassy flats, and a wide river floored with granite cobbles and cold to freeze your kneecaps. Here are ancient Scots pines, and great herds of deer grazing underneath them at dawn, supposing you're awake when you should be. And the Cairngorms are a new country. The mountains are rounded, but huge. Great granite plateaux go on for miles up at the 1000m mark. It's a place to get lost in, or, on a really bad day, to freeze to death in a blizzard.

The following big days can only be treated here in brief. Southeastwards, a long but low-level path leads from Feshie through to Braemar, from whence a natural continuation is by Jock's Road over the Mounth to Glen Clova. Or, northwards you can head out under the pines, for miles and miles, as the Feshie gives way to the Spey. The old railway line of the Speyside Way could even take you right out to the seaside.

Or else you could head on eastward, through the heart of the high Cairngorms. This is backpacking for the tough. Here are vast rocky corries, and wide valleys, and rivers that run brown and dangerous among the dark heather. Here are over a dozen bothies to choose among, and the sublime if squalid Shelter Stone at the head of Loch Avon. And a walk that started at Ben Nevis could well continue under (or over) the UK's second highest, big Ben Macdui.

ROUTE 23
Fort William to Inverie

Start	Fort William (ferry)
Finish	Inverie, Knoydart
Distance	80km (50 miles)
Ascent	1800m (5800ft)
Approximate time	24hr (three good days)
Max altitude	Mam Meadail 555m
Day 1	Road, track and good path
Days 2–3	Tracks and paths, some very small and rough
Facilities	
Fort William (start)	All facilities, rail and coach travel; Camusnagaul ferry www.lochabertransport.org.uk
Glenfinnan	Bunkhouse, hotel, cafés – no shop; trains and Shiel Buses
Inverie	Bunkhouse, hotel; ferry to Mallaig daily, but weather dependent www.westernislescruises.co.uk

For any beginner backpacker, three or four days north to Fort William is a good, tough expedition, and the Great Glen makes a natural end. But the shoulders grow under the rucksack, and three days is scarcely enough for the urban habits to die away, for the eyes to start waking at 5am of their own accord, for the campcraft to become natural so that you enjoy the lochs and mountains instead of worrying about the spoons.

A four-day trip can be a sunshine spell spotted in advance on the Met Office website. But a week will reward you with some real weather, the breeze jostling you into the peat-hole, the patter of raindrops on the tent, the satisfaction of, after two days of drizzle, catching the breeze and getting the sleeping bag dry to its toe-end corners.

To stop in a cosy hostel at Fort William, to drink beer with no thought of how it may affect tomorrow's legs, to put the stinking socks in a plastic bag and knot the top, to watch the peaty grime swirl down the plug hole of the shower, and then stay up late watching some frivolous film – these delights are not to be despised. But even better is to pass through the pedestrian precinct as a wild-booted savage, plundering its goods (but not too much, goods are heavy) while despising its plastic shop signs shutting out the scenery, its pampered car-borne lifeforms, all of them in underwear that's dry…

The obvious way out of William is to walk on along the Great Glen. The Great Glen Way is a true coast-to-coast and is steeped in history to the deep brown colour of a Hostelling Scotland teabag. Well, Coleridge walked it in 1803, the Great Beast Aleister Crowley lived alongside between his early explorations of Kanchenjunga, Thomas Telford built a fascinating canal, plus there's the excitement of not seeing the non-existent Loch Ness Monster for 30 miles all along the side of Loch Ness. But five miles of Thomas Telford's stony towpath is as much as I can put up with, with feet softened by the peat and the heather.

Anyway, there's a better way out of Fort William, which is by water. A school boat fetches the kids in from the empty country in the elbow of Loch Eil. Camusnagaul is ten minutes from the busy town (by boat), about 40 minutes (by road), and approximately 100 years away backwards in terms of time.

It's an easy day, but quite a long one, on a road, a track, and a hill path, right through to Glenfinnan, for a comfortable next night. But north of Glenfinnan is the big country. The next road, a twisty single-track to Kinloch Hourn, is 20 miles away as the eagle flies, and a lot longer than that as the weary walker drags a rucksack. But out to the northwest is a corner where roads are irrelevant. The Knoydart peninsula communicates with the world by boat.

Route 23 – Fort William to Inverie

> Two days of the wildest walking in these islands leads to the tiny pier at Inverie. And it's easier to accept an ending for your foot travel, when the journey continues by that weather-dependent ferry out of Mallaig, and then the West Highland Railway.

DAY 1
Camusnagaul to Glenfinnan

Distance	34km (21½ miles)
Ascent	400m (1300ft)
Approximate time	9hr

The first day's walking is straightforward. The over-excited could head straight up behind **Camusnagaul** ferry pier onto Stob Coire a' Chearcaill – at only 770m it's a mere Corbett, but with the steepness and craggy grass of the West Highlands beyond the Great Glen. For the more gently inclined, there are the gentler inclines of the single-track coast road. After 9km a gravel track leads past **Conaglen House Hotel** into the long, empty Cona Glen.

The next image appears first as a few random pixel squares, then a few more, and spreads. Those who give digital presentations know to avoid such effects if we want to seem even slightly sophisticated. But in **Cona Glen**, above the winding river, this is the way the forest is starting to replace the overgrazed coarse grassland. A few Scots pines here, a clump of birches there, alders by the river – give it

Cona Glen, the track to Glenfinnan

Not the West Highland Way: A Mountain High Way

Mam na Cloiche-airde above Loch Nevis

half a century and we'll suddenly realise we can't see any more the green slopes riven with white watercourses, the grey crags standing against the sky.

From the track's end a quad-bike path slants up to the right, crosses a stream, and then turns up northwest through a pass. From a cairn at the pass top, the path runs down damp in places but mostly good. At **Callop** it joins a track. Cross Allt na Cruaiche to the A830 road. Or take a left turn on the track – only if the river seems shallow enough to paddle, which you'll have to do in another 1.5km.

Follow verges of the slightly busy road to **Glenfinnan**. Glenfinnan is famous as the place where Bonnie Prince Charlie in 1745 first raised the standard of rebellion. It was on 19 August, supported by clansmen of MacDonalds and Camerons, that he claimed the Scottish and English thrones on behalf of his father James Stewart, the event celebrated with bagpiping and brandy. Okay, okay, Glenfinnan is actually famous for the railway viaduct that features in the Harry Potter films, spectacularly in the 'train chases flying Ford Anglia' sequence in Potter 2.

The station has a bunkhouse and dining car, both in old railway carriages, and a small museum. You're now 8km closer to Fort William (by road), but still in a century not the present. The National Trust Visitor Centre feels somewhat nearer to the present day.

DAYS 2–3
Glenfinnan to Inverie

Distance	50km (31 miles)
Ascent	1400m (4500ft)
Approximate time	15hr

You enter the wilderness under the fine **Glenfinnan Viaduct** (okay, 'Hogwarts Bridge'). The **Corryhully bothy** is unusual in having electric light – although the use of a light switch may be inappropriate in this magnificent setting (and anyway your money for the meter is carefully wrapped away inside several plastic bags).

Past **Glenfinnan Lodge** the track degenerates into a soggy path – for best chance of keeping feet dry, divert over the fine Munro Sgurr Thuilm to the left, or the even finer not-quite-Munro Streap on the right. Down in **Glen Dessarry** is another bothy, **A' Chuil**, conveniently placed but somewhat gloomy among its spruce. Glenfinnan to A' Chuil 19km (12 miles), 550m (1800ft), about 6hr.

The map has two paths westwards from A' Chuil and presumably both work: I've only used the northern one, as I like to be out of the plantations.

From here the remaining 25km to Inverie are among the most romantic anywhere, and make south of Fort William seem like a semi-urban parkland. In **Mam na Cloich Airde** the grass and rock rise 800m high, and steep enough to shrug off the 5.5m of annual rainfall. That rain spurts down the sides in streams and

Loch Nevis below Sgurr na Ciche

waterfalls, and gathers in two dark pools that almost block the narrow valley, so that the path edges across the slope foot with one foot in the water. At the pass top, you peer between the raindrops all the way along Loch Nevis.

At the loch head is **Sourlies bothy**. Some people aren't satisfied by the long, empty sea loch going crimson under the sunset; nor by the cry of the eider duck, or the midnight bark of seals; not even by the cragged spire of Sgurr na Ciche overhead. They complain that the bothy chimney smokes a bit. More seriously, because of its extreme distance from where anybody is likely to be, the bothy is often quite crowded… A' Chuil to Sourlies 10km (6½ miles), 150m (500ft), 3–3.5hr.

Leave **Sourlies** on the foreshore, or the awkward hillside above if the tide's in. The crucial footbridge at **Carnoch** has rotted and been replaced, been carried away by a flood and then replaced again. Today, in an intrusion of modern technology that's a new low for mankind in arrogance and intrusiveness – or would be if it wasn't so damned convenient – we can gaze down from Google Earth and verify that, on the last satellite flypast at any rate, this bridge did exist.

Knoydart is not a gentle country – it was nicknamed in Gaelic as the Rough Bounds. The old path climbs 600m to **Mam Meadail** in 2km of westward travel. The mountain slopes around are steeper still. But the descent is gentle, with open sea ahead. The path becomes a track, and the track a strip of tarmac, albeit one not linked to any other road in the world.

The main thing is not to miss the Friday afternoon ferry. Wait in the Old Forge pub for the following boat? It'd be slightly quicker to walk back to Glenfinnan. Sourlies to Inverie 14.5km (9 miles), 650m (2200ft), about 5.5hr.

The island of Rum at 10pm, from Sgurr nan Coireachan above Glenfinnan

ROUTE 24
Spean Bridge to Cluanie and even Cape Wrath

The evening was calm with a slow temperature inversion gradually drawing low mist across the moor below as the lights began to twinkle in the villages along the coast, and on ships in the Minch. With my dinner over it was a delight to sit with glass in hand and watch my cigar smoke drifting slowly from the tent door.
Sandy Cousins on Ganu Mor, Foinaven, on the first night of his walk from Cape Wrath to Glasgow

The ultimate long walk in the UK has been around since 1971, although it only got its name – the Cape Wrath Trail – when a guidebook to it was published by Cicerone in 1999. But the Cape Wrath Trail is a whole lot more interesting even than the guidebook. It is, quite simply, Fort William to Cape Wrath on foot. As well as bemusing you with cooker choices and tent specifications, resupply points and public transport, chiropody and meteorology, navigation and Gaelic nomenclature, the true Trail burdens you with choosing the route. (It also, naturally enough, burdens you with a big rucksack.)

One way north from the Fort is by the Camusnagaul ferry and Glenfinnan, as Route 23. Another way is by the Great Glen. The 11km of Caledonian Canal towpath to Gairlochy is hard work: and dull work too, quite unlike the exhilarating rigours to come. So I prefer to emerge from the southern mountains at Spean Bridge (Route 20).

On Foinaven, last hill south of Cape Wrath

Heading north from Sandwood Bay, with Cape Wrath a day's walk ahead

From the foot of Loch Lochy, the straightforward way north is by Achnacarry and the path up Gleann Cia-aig. It's boggy at the top, with a house called Fedden that must have been a hard one to live in. A new path leads down to plantations, a long bridge across Loch Garry, and the Tomdoun Hotel. Gairlochy to Tomdoun Hotel 29.5km (18½ miles), 400m (1200ft), about 8hr.

A hill path past the head of Loch Loin leads to Cluanie Inn on the A87 (a short day) or the youth hostel at Alltbeithe (a rather long one). And you could continue all the way to the Cape on tracks and paths, with only the odd day or two of pathless inhospitable bog. But those tracks and paths wind among about a hundred of Scotland's finest mountains. Some of those you should certainly aspire to climb.

Then again, direct your course closer to the western sea and you'll get the very finest of sea scenery, the deepest and craggiest valleys, the sharpest and most striking mountains. Keep east and the bogs are less boggy, the hills less steep, the paths somewhat smoother. An eastern route will be about 30 per cent quicker. But then, should you hurry when you're having such fun?

You will see eagles. You may see more eagles than people, as you pass through the rank grassland of Knoydart, that land of the green glens and the stripy grey rocks. You will see the sea from mountaintops, right across to Rum, Skye and the Western Isles, as the sun hits the horizon at 10pm on a midsummer evening. The sea also from close up, as you push the tent pegs into salt marsh next to the brown seaweed, and gather sea-bleached sticks for a fire. During the night the surf rumbles close to the camp and retreats; at dawn you might spot a seal.

ROUTE 24 – SPEAN BRIDGE TO CLUANIE AND EVEN CAPE WRATH

After two or three weeks you pass the last big hill, which is An Teallach. And now the bleak becomes a degree bleaker. Small sandstone mountains stick out like ancient spaceships crashed into the peat before the start of human history. The mountaintop ptarmigans are now met at the hill base. Even the light is whiter, shining off the sea in unexpected directions, through air less stained by man's pollution. The settlement you come to retains the field patterns of primitive Norsemen, and its shop sells nothing you could get at Tesco.

Under Arkle I wake up early because David is squashing me against the side of the tent. Except that when I look, the seam down the tent roof is exactly midway between us. David's tent must be even smaller than I remember. Indeed, as the years go by we need more space to pull our socks on in. This is why less youthful folk need Bigger Tent but at the same time Less Weight. (A tricky equation? Not really. Age, if it brings anything, should surely mean More Money.)

But on this particular May morning, the tent really has got smaller. It has also gone mottled, like turtle soup seen from the inside. This is because the tent has two inches of wet snow on it.

I think about this for five minutes. And work out that the thing to do is to shake the snow off my side of the doorflap. There's a dreadful camping story set on Everest's South Col, a place where the simple choice is to get down or get dead; but, after melting water for tea, heating water for tea, drinking tea, pulling the boots on, there was only enough of the day left to take the boots off again and go back to bed. They'd come up the Kangshung Face – who was it? Yes, Venables.

It's the lack of oxygen that makes you think so slow. I pull myself together, and shake the snow off David's side of the doorflap. Thinking about things doesn't help when the things thought about are low cloud, high wind, and fresh snow on

Sandwood Bay, the last overnight stop before Cape Wrath

the quartzite stonefields of Foinaven. I fold myself into a corner while David does his feet.

'I haven't camped in the snow before,' says David. 'Nasty, isn't it?'

Me, I have camped in the snow before. A Black's Good Companions, full of schoolmates, high in the Lairig Ghru at Easter. In the morning came a nice hot cup of tea in bed. The mug had been used for some particularly greasy stew, and in his eagerness to offer me tea my schoolmate had not had time to wash it up. I crawled into the snow and was sick.

But we haven't just climbed Kangshung and we don't have altitude sickness, so we do eventually get out of the tent. In Sutherland the clouds do rise, the sun does sometimes come. And up on Foinaven, well, there's that speed of the wind where you could fall over under your big sack and break an ankle or two. The wind for us on Foinaven is the crucial five mph less than that.

Foinaven isn't the racehorse, it's spelt differently, and its bones are on view in no Irish stud farm. It's also not a Munro. There was a scare a few years ago, when the OS suddenly discovered an extra 6m that brought it up to 914m. But although 3000ft is 914m, 914m isn't 3000ft but rather 2998ft. Closer survey showed Foinaven not reaching the 914.4m needed by a Munro. Even closer survey suggested the uncertainty in OS measurements allows a one in ten chance that it is actually one after all... No, no, keep quiet about that, Foinaven's very nice indeed as not one. Let the hordes of baggers – sometimes as many in May as two in one day – crowd themselves commuterlike on nearby and somewhat less exciting Ben Hope.

Up on Foinaven it's steep-sided and rocky, breaking out into craggy quartzite. Walking to Cape Wrath means you get to do all Foinaven, end to end. The ridge swoops over six tops, and gets narrow and scrambly. The snow is soft stuff, but good enough to hide the path round the side and give us an Alpine moment down the rocky buttress. Also it does make everything extremely pretty.

Between the main top and the northern one we cross the Moine Thrust for the final time. An arid academic fact about geology? By no means. Moine Thrust means that instead of 2998ft of slippery quartzite blocks to come down on, we get grassy bits and gneiss. Gneiss is grippy to the feet and wavy-textured. Gneiss is nice. And below us is the gneiss moorland, with bare rock and bog grass and dozens of sparkly lochans. At its edge, loch-sprinkled land gives way to island-sprinkled ocean as if Sutherland, and the sea, can't quite work out which is which.

There's a bothy at Sandwood Bay, but we couldn't find it, so we camped down among the dunes. There were a couple of Swedes on the beach as well, but it's a big, big beach. We wandered, watching the light change colour behind the sea-stack called Am Buachaille, and leaving purple-grey footprints on the

Route 24 – Spean Bridge to Cluanie and even Cape Wrath

pinky-golden sand. Then we ate some supper in our sandy hollow, and watched some more colours behind Am Buachaille. During the night the crashing breakers came closer and closer, then died away again down the beach. Urban traffic dies away at midnight, then comes back with the new day. Sandwood sea's the same, but with the volume switch the other way.

Cape Wrath is an ugly spot with its broken concrete buildings, and it was weird when the two minibuses full of birdwatchers suddenly bumbled down the track. That this particular point is a bus stop does seem appropriate. The busman revealed that the rugged outline of the Sandwood Island was down to warplanes with bombs. 'And over there – ' pointing out of the north coast side of the bus, 'is the island they were aiming at. Missed by 12 miles. Not bad, for Americans.' But the driver's a foreigner himself, from faraway Sheffield.

The minibus runs to and fro along a strip of public road split from the rest of Scotland by two miles of sand and water. A ferry takes you across, and in the autumn the bus rejoins the road system on an improvised raft. Meanwhile there's the Durness to Inverness daily, one of the finest bits of public transport in the land. Quinag looked so fine all the way back that I've already bought two more maps and planned a trip across the other way for next year, Helmsdale to Ullapool. Never mind the Highlands. It's the Hills of the North that really rock.

Cape Wrath

APPENDIX A
Access

Since 2005 Scotland has a legal right of access to almost all open country and farmland (the main exceptions being growing crops and land around buildings). Footbridges are explicitly included in the access rights, as are non-damaging cycling, and wild camping – although valley floors in Lomond-Trossach National Park are no-camping. Access must be taken 'responsibly', which means with care for other hill users, land managers and the environment. The full text of the Scottish Access Code is at www.outdooraccess-scotland.scot or by post from Naturescot (the cool new name for Scottish Natural Heritage).

In parts of this area, during the period between mid August (sometimes July) and 21 October, responsible access includes avoiding disturbance to deer-stalking. Hills managed by Scottish Natural Heritage, the National Trust for Scotland and the Forestry Commission are open to walkers year-round. Parts of the area are covered by web information to warn you, around 24 hours in advance, of which hills' deer are under attack – search for 'Heading for the Scottish Hills'. Most of the through routes in Parts Three and Four are on ancient rights of way. In the remaining areas, estates request hillgoers to limit themselves to a small number of specific paths and ridges.

Stalking does not take place on Sundays.

High camp on the north side of Ben Lui (Route 19)

Appendix A – Access

Here are details of the routes in this book where, during those autumn weeks, consideration should be given to stalking activities.

Routes 4 (Beinn a' Choin), 5 (Beinn Chabhair), 6 (Ben Lui) Fyne/Falloch: stalking late August to 20 October, hillwalking@glenfalloch.org.

Route 8 (Beinn Dorain) Auch Estate: stalking first week of September to 20 October. Look out for notices alongside the track. Coire a' Ghabhlaich is prime stalking ground away from usual walkers' routes, and should be avoided during those seven weeks.

Routes 9 (Ben Inverveigh), 10 (Black Mount) Blackmount Partnership: from August to 20 October walkers are asked not to use Route 9. Route 10 (over Creise or Meall a' Bhuiridh) is on the estate's requested routes, but avoid more general wandering during this time.

Route 11 (Beinn a' Chrulaiste) Black Corries Estate: stalking mid Sept to 20 October, blackcorries@googlemail.com.

Route 18 (Arrochar Alps) North from Ben Ime: Fyne/Falloch hillphone, see Route 4. (South of Ben Ime is Forestry Commission.)

Route 19 (Etive Trek) Lui crossing: Fyne/Falloch hillphone, see Route 4. The rest of Route 19 is on rights of way.

Route 21 (Rannoch) A' Chruach is shared between Black Corries Estate (see Route 11) and Rannoch Deer Management Association. The path line marked on OS maps is now mostly a track and is a right of way. The onward route from Rannoch Station to Corrour is a right of way.

Route 22 (Bealach Dubh) is a right of way, but the hills above are stalked by various estates.

Route 23 (Knoydart) is a right of way, but the hills above are stalked by various estates.

Route 24 (to Cluanie Inn) is on rights of way, but the extended trek to Cape Wrath won't work during the stalking season unless you're content to abandon any mountain ambitions – and also to put up with probably pretty nasty weather.

Above Rannoch Moor (crossed by Route 21) on the way up Stob Ghabhar (Route 10)

APPENDIX B
Useful information

Weather
The most useful and accurate Internet forecast is at Mountain Weather Information Systems www.mwis.org.uk. Also good is the Met Office's mountain forecast at www.metoffice.gov.uk/public/weather/mountain-forecast. One or other of these is often posted at hostels and information centres. A webcam for Ben Nevis is at http://visit-fortwilliam.co.uk/webcam/; for Glen Coe, see Meall a'Bhuiridh (or not, if the cloud's down) at www.glencoemountain.co.uk.

Public transport
Journey planner: www.travelinescotland.com tel 0871 200 22 33

The West Highland Railway is one of the treat train rides of the world. And stepping off the freezing night platform at Corrour into the lighted and carpeted compartment is a grand Harry-Potter moment on the line that features in most of his movies (number 6, *The Half-Blood Prince*, takes the train across a digitally manipulated Rannoch Moor). The overview maps at the start of this book show its well-placed stations. There are three services daily, plus the nightly Caledonian Sleeper. See www.scotrail.co.uk tel 08457 48 49 50

The Citylink coaches are cheaper and quicker than the train, and equally scenic. There are at least three daily each way along the A82 Glasgow – Loch Lomond – Crianlarich – Bridge of Orchy – Kings House – Fort William, also Edinburgh – Crianlarich, and Crianlarich – Dalmally – Oban. In the countryside the coach will stop on request wherever it's safe, including at Kings House. See www.citylink.co.uk tel 08705 505050

Accommodation (general)
Hotels, B&Bs, and general information: www.visitscotland.com tel 0845 22 55 121, and www.visitscottishheartlands.com (south of Tyndrum) or www.lochaber.com (further north).
Loch Lomond-Trossachs National Park: www.lochlomond-trossachs.org

Hostelling Scotland (Scottish YHA): www.hostellingscotland.org.uk central bookings tel 0345 293 7373

Independent Hostels:
www.hostel-scotland.co.uk

Campsites:
www.UKcampsite.co.uk

Accommodation and shops (West Highland Way)
(The distance from the start is shown in brackets.)
West Highland Way information at www.west-highland-way.co.uk

Milngavie (0km) Trains to Milngavie from either Glasgow Central or Glasgow Queen Street – in each case from a separate suburban station underneath the main-line one. All facilities, including shops for forgotten gear purchases.

Dumgoyne (12km) Beech Tree Inn, Glengoyne Distillery

NOT THE WEST HIGHLAND WAY: A MOUNTAIN HIGH WAY

Drymen (20km) All facilities including a small outdoor gear shop

Balmaha (32km) Shop, café, pub

Rowardennan (44km) Hotel, youth hostel, bunkhouse, ferry to Tarbet

Rowchoish (50km) Bothy

Inversnaid (55km) Hotel, bunkhouse 1km east up road, ferry to Inveruglas on A82

Doune Byre (51km) Bothy

Ardleish (62km) Ferry to Ardlui on A82

Inverarnan (65km) Drovers' Inn, Beinglas campsite and café with small shop

Crianlarich (75km) Shop, hotels, youth hostel

Auchtertyre (81km) Hostel (wigwams), campsite shop and café

Tyndrum (85km) Hotel, shops (including some outdoor gear), By the Way Hostel, Real Food Café, Green Welly Café

Bridge of Orchy (96km) Hotel, station hostel

Inveroran (100km) Hotel

White Corries (113km) Café

Kings House (115km) Hotel, bunkhouse

Kinlochleven (129km) Hotels, shops; gear shop and café at Ice Factor; Blackwater Hostel; bunk huts at Macdonald Hotel

Glen Nevis (149km) Youth hostel, hostel and pub (Ben Nevis Inn)

Fort William (153km) All facilities

Tourist Information Centres

NOTE: VisitScotland have decided to close all their iCentres by 2026. So the Balloch and Fort William centres listed below may not be available throughout the lifespan of this guide.

Balloch, Old Station
tel 01389 753533

Balmaha, National Park Centre
tel 01389 722100

Ballachulish Information Centre, Glen Coe
tel 01855 811866

Kinlochleven, www.kinlochleven.org.uk

Ben Nevis Visitor Centre, Glen Nevis
tel 01349 781401

Fort William, 15 High St, PH33 6DH
tel 01397 701801

APPENDIX C
Further reading

West Highland Way

West Highland Way by Roger Smith (Mercat Press 9th edition 2010) or the original West Highland Way Official Guide by Robert Aitken (HMSO 1980).

The West Highland Way by Terry Marsh (Cicerone 5th edition 2024) Includes a separate map booklet with full OS 1:25,000 maps of the route.

The West Highland Way by Ronald Turnbull (Frances Lincoln 2010) A picture book with a smattering of history and wildlife.

Wider guidebooks

The Highland High Way by Heather Connon and Paul Roper (Mainstream 1996, out of print). A 'Not the WH Way' in all but name, using WH Way overnight points and taking the highest and most energetic mountain routes between them, crossing 25 Munros (the maximum Munros using routes in Part One of this book is 13).

Walking the Munros Vol 1 by Steve Kew (Cicerone 4th edition 2021). All the 3000ft summits in the Southern Highlands, by their popular standard routes.

The Central Highlands: Six Long-distance Walks by Peter Koch-Osborne (Cicerone 1998, out of print). Expands outwards from the Not the WH Way routes here, with glen walks on good paths and tracks: from Taynuilt to Dalwhinnie, a network over Rannoch Moor, and an excursion from Drymen northeastwards to Glen Almond.

Backpackers' Britain Vol 4: Central and Southern Scottish Highlands by Graham Uney (Cicerone 2008, out of print). More ambitious backpacking taking in high mountain ridges.

The Cape Wrath Trail by Iain Harper (Cicerone 4th edition 2022). The full 21-day walk from Fort William to Cape Wrath on tracks, paths and the odd bog, not crossing any summits. Their route starts the good way, over the Camusnagaul ferry.

Walking Loch Lomond and the Trossachs by Ronald Turnbull (Cicerone 2nd edition 2018). Full walkers' guide to mountains, lower hills, and valley routes in the National Park, north to Tyndrum.

Ben Nevis and Glen Coe by Ronald Turnbull (Cicerone 2nd edition 2016). Full walkers' guide to mountains, lower hills, and valley routes north and west from Inveroran to the Great Glen.

History and fiction

Rob Roy Macgregor: his Life and Times by WH Murray (Canongate 1982). Scholarly and readable, and includes general matter on Macgregor hiking exploits.

Rob Roy (film) directed by Michael Caton Jones (1995), starring Liam Neeson, Jessica Lange, John Hurt, Tim Roth. History or fiction? A surprising amount is historically based, the scenery is splendid and so are the villains.

NOT THE WEST HIGHLAND WAY: A MOUNTAIN HIGH WAY

Rob Roy by Sir Walter Scott (1817, many paperback editions). Adventures along the side of Loch Lomond, with a long and authoritative historical introduction.

Glencoe: the Story of the Massacre by John Prebble (Penguin 1968). An account that's vivid and moving, but scholarly as well; the complicated politics, the drama and sadness, plus general hiking exploits of the MacDonalds.

Recollections of a Tour Made in Scotland by Dorothy Wordsworth (1803, included in *Dorothy Wordsworth: a Longman Cultural Edition* ed Susan Levin). Most of the WH Way, plus Glen Coe and some poetry.

Coleridge among the Lakes and Mountains (Folio Society 1991, available second-hand). The poet walked much of the WH Way and the Great Glen Way in 1803, as well as in Somerset and the Lake District.

Hostile Habitats: Scotland's Mountain Environment (SMT with Scottish Natural Heritage). A useful, well-illustrated guide to wildlife and landforms.

The West Highland Railway by David St John Thomas (David & Charles 1965). On Rannoch Moor, a train-spotter's anorak is actually an essential, as the seven surveyors with their umbrellas discovered in 1889. Fascinating stories of bottomless bogs, runaway trains and lethal hillwalks out of Corrour; almost no numbers copied off the fronts of trains.

Kidnapped by Robert Louis Stevenson (1886). Would be Scotland's finest historical adventure even if it didn't involve a long-distance walk across Rannoch Moor.

John Splendid by Neil Munro (1898). A fairly gripping historical romance featuring a lost walker on Rannoch Moor (Route 21) as well as Montrose's winter raid along Route 20. It is written, intriguingly, from a pro-Campbell point of view.

Narrow Road to the Deep North by Basho, translated by Noboyuki Yuasa (Penguin, originally published 1689). 'Every day is a journey, and the journey itself is home.'

The Fleming memorial stands above the track of the West Highland Way; across Rannoch Moor to Beinn an Dothaidh

NOTES

DOWNLOAD THE GPX FILES

All the routes in this guide are available for download from:

www.cicerone.co.uk/1187/GPX

as standard format GPX files. You should be able to load them into most online GPX systems and mobile devices, whether GPS or smartphone. You may need to convert the file into your preferred format using a conversion programme such as gpsvisualizer.com or one of the many other such websites and programmes.

When you follow this link, you will be asked for your email address and where you purchased the guidebook, and have the option to subscribe to the Cicerone e-newsletter.

www.cicerone.co.uk

LISTING OF CICERONE GUIDES

BRITISH ISLES CHALLENGES, COLLECTIONS AND ACTIVITIES

Great Walks on the England Coast Path
Map and Compass
The Big Rounds
The Book of the Bivvy
The Book of the Bothy
The Mountains of England and Wales:
  Vol 1 Wales
  Vol 2 England
The National Trails
Walking the End to End Trail
Cycling Land's End to John o' Groats

SHORT WALKS SERIES

15 Short Walks Hadrian's Wall
15 Short Walks in the Lake District: Keswick, Borrowdale and Buttermere
15 Short Walks in the Lake District: Windermere Ambleside and Grasmere
15 Short Walks Lake District: Coniston and Langdale
15 Short Walks in Arnside and Silverdale
15 Short Walks in the Ribble Valley
15 Short Walks in Nidderdale
15 Short Walks in Northumberland: Wooler, Rothbury, Alnwick and the coast
15 Short Walks in the Yorkshire Dales: Grassington, Skipton, Malham and Ilkley
15 Short Walks in the Peak District: Bakewell and the White Peak
15 Short Walks on the Malvern Hills
15 Short Walks in Cornwall: Falmouth and the Lizard
15 Short Walks in Cornwall: Land's End and Penzance
15 Short Walks in the South Downs: Brighton, Eastbourne and Arundel
15 Short Walks in the Surrey Hills
15 Short Walks on Dartmoor North: Okehampton and Chagford
15 Short Walks on Dartmoor South: Ivybridge and Princetown
15 Short Walks on Exmoor
15 Short Walks Winchester
15 Short Walks in Bannau Brycheiniog: Brecon Beacons
15 Short Walks in Pembrokeshire: Tenby and the south
15 Short Walks in Dumfries and Galloway
15 Short Walks in the Trossachs: Callander and Aberfoyle
15 Short Walks on the Isle of Mull
15 Short Walks on the Orkney Islands
15 Short Walks on the Shetland Islands

SCOTLAND

Ben Nevis and Glen Coe
Cycling in the Hebrides
Cycling the North Coast 500
Great Mountain Days in Scotland
Mountain Biking in Southern and Central Scotland
Mountain Biking in West and North West Scotland
Not the West Highland Way: A Mountain High Way
Scotland
Scotland's Best Small Mountains
Scotland's Mountain Ridges
Scottish Wild Country Backpacking
Skye's Cuillin Ridge Traverse
The Borders Abbeys Way
The Great Glen Way
The Great Glen Way Map Booklet
The Hebridean Way
The Hebrides
The Isle of Mull
The Isle of Skye
The Skye Trail
The Southern Upland Way
The West Highland Way
The West Highland Way Map Booklet
Walking Ben Lawers, Rannoch and Atholl
Walking in the Cairngorms
Walking in the Pentland Hills
Walking in the Scottish Borders
Walking in the Southern Uplands
Walking in Torridon, Fisherfield, Fannichs and An Teallach
Walking Loch Lomond and the Trossachs
Walking on Arran
Walking on Harris and Lewis
Walking on Jura, Islay and Colonsay
Walking on Mull, Coll and Tiree
Walking on Rum and the Small Isles
Walking on the Orkney and Shetland Isles
Walking on Uist and Barra
Walking the Cape Wrath Trail
Walking the Corbetts
  Vol 1 South of the Great Glen
  Vol 2 North of the Great Glen
Walking the Fife Pilgrim Way
Walking the Galloway Hills
Walking the John o' Groats Trail
Walking the Munros
  Vol 1 Southern, Central and Western Highlands
  Vol 2 Northern Highlands and the Cairngorms
Winter Climbs in the Cairngorms
Winter Climbs: Ben Nevis and Glen Coe

NORTHERN ENGLAND ROUTES

Cycling the Reivers Route
Cycling the Way of the Roses
Hadrian's Cycleway
Hadrian's Wall Path
Hadrian's Wall Path Map Booklet
The Coast to Coast Cycle Route
The Coast to Coast Map Booklet
The Coast to Coast Walk
Walking the Dales Way
The Dales Way Map Booklet
Walking the Pennine Way
Pennine Way Map Booklet

LAKE DISTRICT

Bikepacking in the Lake District
Cycling in the Lake District
Great Mountain Days in the Lake District
Joss Naylor's Lakes, Meres and Waters of the Lake District
Lake District Winter Climbs
Lake District:
  High Level and Fell Walks
  Low Level and Lake Walks
Mountain Biking in the Lake District
Outdoor Adventures with Children — Lake District
Scrambles in the Lake District —
  North
  South
Trail and Fell Running in the Lake District
Walking The Cumbria Way
Walking the Lake District Fells —
  Borrowdale
  Buttermere
  Coniston
  Keswick
  Langdale
  Mardale and the Far East
  Patterdale
  Wasdale
Walking the Tour of the Lake District

NORTH-WEST ENGLAND AND THE ISLE OF MAN

Cycling the Pennine Bridleway
Isle of Man Coastal Path
The Lancashire Cycleway
The Lune Valley and Howgills
Walking in Cumbria's Eden Valley
Walking in Lancashire
Walking in the Forest of Bowland and Pendle
Walking on the Isle of Man
Walking on the West Pennine Moors
Walking the Ribble Way
Walks in Silverdale and Arnside

NORTH-EAST ENGLAND, YORKSHIRE DALES AND PENNINES

Cycling in the Yorkshire Dales
Great Mountain Days in the Pennines
Mountain Biking in the Yorkshire Dales
The Cleveland Way and the Yorkshire Wolds Way
The Cleveland Way Map Booklet
The North York Moors
Trail and Fell Running in the Yorkshire Dales
Walking in County Durham
Walking in Northumberland
Walking in the North Pennines
Walking in the Yorkshire Dales:
   North and East
   South and West
Walking St Cuthbert's Way
Walking St Oswald's Way and Northumberland Coast Path

DERBYSHIRE, PEAK DISTRICT AND MIDLANDS

Cycling in the Peak District
Dark Peak Walks
Scrambles in the Dark Peak
Walking in Derbyshire
Walking in the Peak District -
   White Peak East
   White Peak West

WALES AND WELSH BORDERS

Cycle Touring in Wales
Cycling Lon Las Cymru
Great Mountain Days in Snowdonia
Hillwalking in Shropshire
Mountain Walking in Snowdonia
Offa's Dyke Path
Offa's Dyke Map Booklet
Scrambles in Snowdonia
Snowdonia: 30 Low-level and Easy Walks — North, South
The Cambrian Way
The Pembrokeshire Coast Path
The Pembrokeshire Coast Path Map Booklet
The Snowdonia Way
The Wye Valley Walk
Walking Glyndwr's Way
Walking in Carmarthenshire
Walking in Pembrokeshire
Walking in the Brecon Beacons
Walking in the Wye Valley
Walking on Gower
Walking the Severn Way
Walking the Shropshire Way
Walking the Wales Coast Path

SOUTHERN ENGLAND

20 Classic Sportive Rides
   in South East England
   in South West England
Cycling in the Cotswolds
Mountain Biking on the North Downs
Mountain Biking on the South Downs
The North Downs Way
The North Downs Way Map Booklet
The South Downs Way
The South Downs Way Map Booklet
The Cotswold Way
The Cotswold Way Map Booklet
The Ridgeway National Trail
The Ridgeway Map Booklet
The Thames Path
The Thames Path Map Booklet
The Two Moors Way
Two Moors Way Map Booklet
Walking the South West Coast Path
South West Coast Path Map Booklet
   Vol 1: Minehead to St Ives
   Vol 2: St Ives to Plymouth
   Vol 2: St Ives to Plymouth
   Vol 3: Plymouth to Poole
Suffolk Coast and Heath Walks
The Kennet and Avon Canal
The Lea Valley Walk
The Peddars Way and Norfolk Coast Path
The Pilgrims' Way
Walking Hampshire's Test Way
Walking in Essex
Walking in Kent
Walking in London
Walking in Norfolk
Walking in the Chilterns
Walking in the Cotswolds
Walking in the Isles of Scilly
Walking in the New Forest
Walking in the North Wessex Downs
Walking on Dartmoor
Walking on Guernsey
Walking on Jersey
Walking on the Isle of Wight
Walking the Dartmoor Way
Walking the Jurassic Coast
Walking the Sarsen Way
Walks in the South Downs National Park

ALPS CROSS-BORDER ROUTES

100 Hut Walks in the Alps
Alpine Ski Mountaineering Vol 1 — Western Alps
The Karnischer Hohenweg
The Tour of the Bernina
Trail Running — Chamonix and the Mont Blanc region
Trekking Chamonix to Zermatt
Trekking in the Alps
Trekking in the Silvretta and Ratikor Alps
Trekking Munich to Venice
Trekking the Tour du Mont Blanc
Tour du Mont Blanc Map Booklet
Walking in the Alps

FRANCE, BELGIUM, AND LUXEMBOURG

Camino de Santiago — Via Podiensis
Chamonix Mountain Adventures
Cycling London to Paris
Cycling the Canal de la Garonne
Cycling the Canal du Midi
Mont Blanc Walks
Mountain Adventures in the Maurienne
Short Treks on Corsica
The GR5 Trail
The GR5 Trail —
   Vosges and Jura
   Benelux and Lorraine
The Moselle Cycle Route
Trekking in the Vanoise
Trekking the Cathar Way
Trekking the GR10
Trekking the GR20 Corsica
Trekking the Robert Louis Stevenson Trail
Via Ferratas of the French Alps
Walking in Provence — East
Walking in Provence — West
Walking in the Auvergne
Walking in the Briançonnais
Walking in the Dordogne
Walking in the Haute Savoie: North
Walking in the Haute Savoie: South
Walking on Corsica
Walking the Brittany Coast Path
Walking in the Ardennes

PYRENEES AND FRANCE/SPAIN CROSS-BORDER ROUTES

Shorter Treks in the Pyrenees
The Pyrenean Haute Route
The Pyrenees
Trekking the Cami dels Bons Homes
Trekking the GR11 Trail
Walks and Climbs in the Pyrenees

SPAIN AND PORTUGAL

Camino de Santiago: Camino Frances
Coastal Walks in Andalucia
Costa Blanca Mountain Adventures
Cycling the Camino de Santiago
Mountain Walking in Mallorca
Mountain Walking in Southern Catalunya
Spain's Sendero Historico: The GR1
The Andalucian Coast to Coast Walk
The Camino del Norte and Camino Primitivo
The Camino Ingles and Ruta do Mar
The Mountains Around Nerja
The Mountains of Ronda and Grazalema
The Sierras of Extremadura
Trekking in Mallorca
Trekking in the Canary Islands
Trekking the GR7 in Andalucia
Walking and Trekking in the Sierra Nevada
Walking in Andalucia
Walking in Catalunya —
   Barcelona
   Girona Pyrenees
Walking in the Picos de Europa
Walking La Via de la Plata and Camino Sanabres
Walking on Gran Canaria
Walking on La Gomera and El Hierro

Walking on La Palma
Walking on Lanzarote and Fuerteventura
Walking on Tenerife
Walking on the Costa Blanca
Walking the Camino dos Faros
Portugal's Rota Vicentina
The Camino Portugues
Walking in Portugal
Walking in the Algarve
Walking on Madeira
Walking on the Azores

SWITZERLAND
Switzerland's Jura Crest Trail
The Swiss Alps
Tour of the Jungfrau Region
Trekking the Swiss Via Alpina
Walking in Arolla and Zinal
Walking in the Bernese Oberland — Jungfrau region
Walking in the Engadine — Switzerland
Walking in Ticino
Walking in Zermatt and Saas-Fee

GERMANY
Hiking and Cycling in the Black Forest
The Danube Cycleway Vol 1
The Rhine Cycle Route
The Westweg
Walking in the Bavarian Alps

POLAND, SLOVAKIA, ROMANIA, HUNGARY AND BULGARIA
The Danube Cycleway Vol 2
The High Tatras
The Mountains of Romania

SCANDINAVIA, ICELAND AND GREENLAND
Hiking in Norway —
  North
  South
Trekking the Kungsleden
Trekking in Greenland — The Arctic Circle Trail
Walking and Trekking in Iceland

SLOVENIA, CROATIA, SERBIA, MONTENEGRO AND ALBANIA
Hiking Slovenia's Juliana Trail
Mountain Biking in Slovenia
The Islands of Croatia
The Julian Alps of Slovenia
The Mountains of Montenegro
The Peaks of the Balkans Trail
The Peaks of the Balkans Trail
The Slovene Mountain Trail
Walking in Slovenia: The Karavanke
Walks and Treks in Croatia

ITALY
Alta Via
  1 — Trekking in the Dolomites
  2 — Trekking in the Dolomites

Day Walks in the Dolomites
Italy's Grande Traversata delle Alpi
Italy's Sibillini National Park
Ski Touring and Snowshoeing in the Dolomites
The Way of St Francis: Via di Francesco
Trekking Gran Paradiso: Alta Via 2
Trekking in the Apennines
Trekking the Giants' Trail: Alta Via 1 through the Italian Pennine Alps
Via Ferratas of the Italian Dolomites:
  Vol 1
  Vol 2
Walking in Abruzzo
Walking in Italy's Cinque Terre
Walking in Italy's Stelvio National Park
Walking in Sicily
Walking in the Aosta Valley
Walking in the Dolomites
Walking in Tuscany
Walking in Umbria
Walking Lake Como and Maggiore
Walking Lake Garda and Iseo
Walking on the Amalfi Coast
Walking the Via Francigena Pilgrim Route
  Part 1
  Part 2
  Part 3
  Part 4
Walks and Treks in the Maritime Alps

IRELAND
The Wild Atlantic Way and Western Ireland
Walking the Kerry Way
Walking the Wicklow Way

EUROPEAN CYCLING
Cycling the Route des Grandes Alpes
Cycling the Ruta Via de la Plata
The Elbe Cycle Route
The River Loire Cycle Route
The River Rhone Cycle Route

INTERNATIONAL CHALLENGES, COLLECTIONS AND ACTIVITIES
Europe's High Points
Pocket First Aid and Wilderness Medicine

AUSTRIA
Innsbruck Mountain Adventures
Trekking Austria's Adlerweg
Trekking in Austria's Hohe Tauern
Trekking in Austria's Stubai Alps
Trekking in Austria's Zillertal Alps
Walking in Austria
Walking in the Salzkammergut: the Austrian Lake District

MEDITERRANEAN
The High Mountains of Crete
Trekking in Greece
Walking and Trekking in Zagori
Walking and Trekking on Corfu

Walking on the Greek Islands — the Cyclades
Walking in Cyprus
Walking on Malta

HIMALAYA
8000 metres
Everest: A Trekker's Guide
Trekking in the Karakoram

NORTH AMERICA
Hiking and Cycling the California Missions Trail
Hiking the Pacific Crest Trail
The John Muir Trail

SOUTH AMERICA
Aconcagua and the Southern Andes
Hiking and Biking Peru's Inca Trails
Trekking in Torres del Paine

AFRICA
Climbing Toubkal
Kilimanjaro
Walking in the Drakensberg
Walks and Scrambles in the Moroccan Anti-Atlas

NEW ZEALAND AND AUSTRALIA
Hiking the Overland Track

CHINA, JAPAN AND ASIA
Annapurna
Hiking and Trekking in the Japan Alps and Mount Fuji
Hiking in Hong Kong
Japan's Kumano Kodo Pilgrimage
Japan's Kumano Kodo Pilgrimage
Trekking in Bhutan
Trekking in Ladakh
Trekking in Tajikistan
Trekking in the Himalaya

TECHNIQUES
Fastpacking
The Mountain Hut Book

MINI GUIDES
Alpine Flowers
Navigation

MOUNTAIN LITERATURE
A Walk in the Clouds
Abode of the Gods
Fifty Years of Adventure
The Pennine Way — the Path, the People, the Journey
Unjustifiable Risk?

For full information on all our guides, books and eBooks, visit our website:
www.cicerone.co.uk

CICERONE

Trust Cicerone to guide your next adventure, wherever it may be around the world...

Discover guides for hiking, mountain walking, backpacking, trekking, trail running, cycling and mountain biking, ski touring, climbing and scrambling in Britain, Europe and worldwide.

Connect with Cicerone online and find inspiration.

- buy books and ebooks
- articles, advice and trip reports
- GPX files and updates
- regular newsletter

cicerone.co.uk